Cloud Computing Using Oracle Application Express

Develop Internet-Facing Business Applications Accessible Anywhere and Anytime

Second Edition

Riaz Ahmed

Apress®

Cloud Computing Using Oracle Application Express: Develop Internet-Facing Business Applications Accessible Anywhere and Anytime

Riaz Ahmed
Karachi, Pakistan

ISBN-13 (pbk): 978-1-4842-4242-1   ISBN-13 (electronic): 978-1-4842-4243-8
https://doi.org/10.1007/978-1-4842-4243-8

Library of Congress Control Number: 2018964483

Managing Director, Apress Media LLC: Welmoed Spahr
Acquisitions Editor: Celestin Suresh John
Development Editor: Matthew Moodie
Coordinating Editor: Shrikant Vishwakarma

Cover designed by eStudioCalamar

Cover image designed by Freepik (www.freepik.com)

Distributed to the book trade worldwide by Springer Science+Business Media New York, 233 Spring Street, 6th Floor, New York, NY 10013. Phone 1-800-SPRINGER, fax (201) 348-4505, e-mail orders-ny@springer-sbm.com, or visit www.springeronline.com. Apress Media, LLC is a California LLC and the sole member (owner) is Springer Science + Business Media Finance Inc (SSBM Finance Inc). SSBM Finance Inc is a **Delaware** corporation.

For information on translations, please e-mail rights@apress.com, or visit http://www.apress.com/rights-permissions.

Apress titles may be purchased in bulk for academic, corporate, or promotional use. eBook versions and licenses are also available for most titles. For more information, reference our Print and eBook Bulk Sales web page at http://www.apress.com/bulk-sales.

Any source code or other supplementary material referenced by the author in this book is available to readers on GitHub via the book's product page, located at www.apress.com/978-1-4842-4242-1. For more detailed information, please visit http://www.apress.com/source-code.

Printed on acid-free paper

Table of Contents

TABLE OF CONTENTS

About the Author

Riaz Ahmed is an IT professional with more than 25 years of experience. He started his career in early 90's as a programmer and has been employed in a wide variety of information technology positions, including analyst programmer, system analyst, project manager, data architect, database designer, and senior database administrator. His core areas of interest include web-based development technologies, business intelligence, and databases.

Riaz possesses extensive experience in database design and development. Besides all versions of Oracle, he has worked intensively in almost all major RDBMS on the market today. During his career, he has designed and implemented numerous databases for a wide range of applications, including ERP.

About the Technical Reviewers

Ashish Sinha, a software developer with more than 5 years of experience, has extensive working knowledge of Web Technologies and Oracle Cloud Services. His areas of expertise include various versions of Oracle Apex utilizing jQuery, JavaScript, and Oracle Databases.

Ashish hails from City of Nawabs, Lucknow and currently lives in Silicon Valley of India, Bangalore. He enjoys playing TT, badminton, and swimming.

Ashlesh Patil is a highly motivated and results-driven individual with 5+ years of IT experience in Architecture, Development, and Delivery.

His passion for technology and solutions and program delivery, together with expert skills in development, integration, performance, and security, allows him to contribute a unique blend of business, technical, and process skills across a variety of applications and platforms to deliver time- and cost-effective solutions and business results.

Capabilities: Solution and designs, Integration Architecture.

Development skills: Oracle Application Express (Apex),OAF,PL-SQL,Oracle Information Discovery,Web-services,Oracle RICE Components ,Workflows, Integration Services ,Oracle Forms, Oracle Information Discovery.

Oracle Modules Worked: Oracle Inventory, Human Resource Management System (HRMS), Oracle Financials for India (GST), E business Tax (EBT), Complex Maintenance Repair and Overhaul (CMRO).

Introduction

This is a next-level Oracle APEX book that is written for intermediate users who possess some working knowledge of Oracle APEX. Besides providing new development techniques, it equips the audience with the domain knowledge they need to develop real-world business apps for and in the cloud. Oracle APEX has made the lives of web developers much easier. This rapid application development platform helps you create web-based, data-centric applications easily and instantly without writing tons of code.

You might be one of those readers who is already familiar with Oracle APEX, having some experience in developing simple applications but lacking the required knowledge that is needed to develop a comprehensive system. In this book you will bridge this gap by developing a complete general ledger accounting system named The Cloud Accountant, which will be accessible through a variety of devices including desktops, laptops, and the latest smartphones. Besides the development of a functional application (which you can deploy in your organization or even in other organizations to earn some handsome bucks), the book teaches lots of new techniques to further enhance your APEX development skills.

CHAPTER 1

Introduction to Cloud Computing and the Application Project

The phenomenal growth of information technology—especially the advent of cloud computing—is changing the landscape of information technology, business, and personal computing. If applied correctly, it can increase the productivity of enterprises and enable them to focus on increasing profits and lowering costs. Cloud computing in its simplest form means accessing and storing data and applications over the Internet, instead of on a native computer's hard drive. The purpose of this book is to give you a taste of cloud computing by developing a functional general ledger accounting system for and in the cloud.

1.1 An Introduction to Cloud Computing

Swift adaptation is the key to success for the survival of any business in today's dynamic economic environment. If one is running a profitable business today, this doesn't mean that the current business model will provide the same growth in the future. In addition to adapting to changing government regulations, businesses must explore and implement new areas to cope with current IT trends. In this book, you will be given a taste of cloud computing, which provides an effective computing infrastructure for today's business whenever or wherever it is needed.

1

© Riaz Ahmed 2019
R. Ahmed, *Cloud Computing Using Oracle Application Express*,
https://doi.org/10.1007/978-1-4842-4243-8_1

Many businesses have already switched their IT resources to the cloud because, according to them, this model delivers a more cost-effective and efficient way to serve their customers, partners, and suppliers. In contrast, there are many businesses that are looking at this model more cautiously with respect to the security of their business processes and intellectual assets. The biggest advantage provided by cloud computing is that it eliminates many of the complex constraints found in the traditional computing environment, including cost, space, time, and power.

The following are the three main types of cloud services being delivered by various cloud service providers:

- *Infrastructure as a Service (IaaS)*: In this type, the service provider delivers computer hardware (servers, operating systems, virtualization technology, networking technology, and storage) as a service. Amazon's Elastic Compute Cloud (Amazon EC2) is a good example of IaaS in which a web interface is provided to customers to access virtual machines.

- *Platform as a Service (PaaS)*: This layer offers development environments to IT organizations to develop Internet-facing cloud applications.

- *Software as a Service (SaaS)*: This is one of the first implementations of cloud services where a service provider hosts business applications in its own vicinity and delivers them to its customers.

1.2 Public vs. Private Cloud

The primary objective of designing applications in Oracle Application Express (APEX) is that these applications are accessible anywhere and at any time. APEX, hence, neatly supports cloud computing. To achieve this objective, you are provided with the following two cloud deployment models to host your applications:

Public cloud: A public cloud is a computing model wherein a service provider provides computing resources to the general public over the Internet. These resources include hardware, networks, storage, services, and applications. Public cloud services may be free or offered on a pay-per-usage model. Some companies (including the Oracle Corporation) offer a database cloud service, which has two main components: *RESTful web service access* (which allows access to the data in your database cloud service through simple URIs) and *Oracle Application Express* (for creating and deploying all kinds of applications in a browser-based environment). The database cloud service is simple to obtain, simple to administer, and simple to use to develop and deploy all types of applications. This simplicity is complemented by a simple pricing structure, based on only two metrics: storage and data transfer. In addition, the simplicity of the public cloud means lower costs for your own IT staff. Universal access to the components of the public cloud through a browser dramatically simplifies the maintenance overhead for your cloud-based solutions. Applications delivered through the public cloud can be accessed from a wide variety of client platforms, including Windows, Apple, or mobile devices. Oracle Corporation provides its own cloud computing platform called Oracle Cloud. For further details, see `https://cloud.oracle.com`.

Private cloud: This term refers to the data centers inside your company's firewall. Within your organization you can have a single Oracle Database supporting many departments, with each having their own workspaces to build applications. Each of these workspaces can be granted access to one or more schemas as appropriate. The term may also apply to a private space dedicated to your company within a cloud provider's data center. Private clouds enable organizations to have complete control and visibility over security, regulatory compliance, service levels, and functionality.

Oracle APEX applications are built on technology that resides within an Oracle Database, so all your applications can be easily run on any Oracle platform, from the Oracle Database Cloud Service to your in-house data center to Oracle Database XE on your laptop. Once you have developed an application either on your PC or in the cloud, simply export the application and then import into any other Oracle Database where you have a compatible version of APEX installed. Naturally you may also deploy your application on the Oracle Database Cloud Service and then allow access to it from anywhere in the world.

1.3 What Is Accounting?

Since you will be developing an accounting application in the upcoming chapters, it is necessary to have a little background of accounting. Accounting can be defined as follows: the systematic recording, reporting, and analysis of financial transactions of a business. Accounting provides financial information to stakeholders. Stakeholders include banks, suppliers, investors, government agencies, and people engaged with an organization, such as its owners and employees. Banks need financial information to assess the condition of a firm before lending money. A profitable organization with positive cash flows can easily acquire loans as compared to one suffering heavy losses and little money. Suppliers need financial information to consider trade credit. Investors will invest their money only in profitable organizations. They determine the profitability of an organization by reading its financial statements. Every business concern is bound by law to report on its revenue and expenses to local government agencies for income tax purposes. In a nutshell, accounting performs the following tasks:

- Evaluates profit or loss of a business concern

- Provides detailed information about a firm's net worth

- Reports on assets, liabilities, owner's equity, and profitability

1.4 Accounting System

Organizations use accounting systems (either manual or computerized) to store, manage, and provide their financial information to their stakeholders. These systems are implemented to produce financial statements, including income statement, balance sheet, and other accounting reports. They store detailed records of accounts, such as cash, accounts receivable (due from customers), accounts payable (due to suppliers/ banks), fixed assets, stocks, and so on. This book will teach you how to develop a computerized accounting system to store the financial information of a fictitious company in an organized manner and will provide instructions for creating all the generic financial reports that will be produced with a mouse click.

1.5 General Ledger

In enterprise resource planning (ERP) software, the general ledger module works as a central repository for accounting data transferred from other modules such as fixed assets, product planning, material purchasing, inventory control, distribution, marketing, and HR. A general ledger carries all the accounts for recording financial transactions relating to a company's assets, liabilities, owners' equity, revenues, and expenses. It is known as the backbone of any accounting system because it ties together all of the component transaction processing cycles and systems in an organization.

A sound general ledger system has the following broad objectives:

- Recording of all accounting transactions promptly and accurately

- Posting of transactions to the proper accounts

- Maintaining an equality of debit and credit balances among the accounts

- Generating reliable and timely financial reports for stakeholders

The following are the major functions performed by a general ledger system:

- *Data collection*: Business transactions arise when some sale or purchase event occurs. In the real world, these transactions are handled by their respective operation processing systems, such as sales and purchase systems. These systems interface with the general ledger system in order to feed their daily transactions. Transactions arising from other sources are recorded though specially designed forms, called vouchers. You will use the latter method in this book for transaction processing.

- *Classification and coding*: For proper maintenance of accounts, daily transactions are classified and coded according to a prescribed chart of accounts.

- *Validation*: To ascertain the accuracy of data, every transaction goes through a process of validation that is implemented through various control procedures. These validations include checks on amounts, use of valid account codes from the chart of accounts, transaction period verification, and so on.

- *Reporting*: A general ledger system provides three primary financial statements: income statement, the balance sheet, and a statement of cash flows. While the most familiar financial outputs are the financial statements, numerous other reports (e.g., trial balance, ledgers, budget variance reports, etc.) are also generated by a general ledger system to fulfill the information requirements of the stakeholders.

1.6 The Cloud Accountant General Ledger Project

Running your business gets a whole lot easier when you can access your books anywhere and anytime. The Cloud Accountant being developed in this book is a complete double-entry cloud accounting application that lets you keep in touch with your business all the time. The intensely competitive market in today's economy requires that managers continuously improve the way they work and make decisions. Today's successful managers demand instantaneous information that is both accurate and useful. A traditional desktop accounting system simply cannot cope with these high demands. Only by taking advantage of the power of the latest technology can these demands be met.

The goal of the Cloud Accountant is to remove most of the boring bookkeeping work from the business. The application will take over all the simple and monotonous tasks that can eat up precious time. For instance, it will automate all period-end tasks such as closing the books, transferring the closing balances forward, and so on, with just a few clicks. It also facilitates the recording of all purchase and sales transactions, bill payments, and so on. Since the application can process and retrieve business transactions instantly, there will be a quicker response time to customers, suppliers, and creditors, which will ensure better business relations. In addition, it will produce professional-looking financial reports and accounting records quickly and easily. The Cloud Accountant will free up more time, which can be used to work on improving other areas of the business.

A paperless environment means less work and less confusion since all information is stored electronically and can be accessed instantaneously. A computerized system will also produce more accurate records. The logic created in this application ensures that all entries are posted properly and that the calculations of key financial data are done correctly. This greatly reduces the potential for human error that is prevalent in manual accounting systems. Because of the inherent structure within the Cloud Accountant, the accounting system around the computer will be simplified and more organized. As a result, the flow of information in all stages of the business cycle will be more logical and efficient. Of great importance are the security features built into the application, which ensure that only authorized people have access to company's sensitive financial information. In this application, you will define your own security levels that will allow users to access only what you want them to access. This ensures that data will remain safe, can be easily maintained, and is neat and organized.

1.7 Development Environment

Although you can develop the application locally on your own PC, it is a good idea to develop it in the cloud. This way, not only will you enjoy the latest version (APEX 18.1), but you will also have a complete infrastructure provided by Oracle available for you. Create a free workspace on `https://apex.oracle.com`. After creating the workspace, create a new desktop database application, which will contain Home and Login pages by default. My application is named the Cloud Accountant, and I associated it with a new schema named GL. I selected Universal Theme (42) for the application and for the time being set Authentication Scheme for the application to the default APEX Accounts scheme. Later you will create a custom authentication scheme to implement a custom authentication and application access mechanism.

1.8 Application Segments

Table 1-1 lists all the segments of this application you will develop in this book.

Table 1-1. *Application Segments*

Menu	Application Segment	APEX Page Number
Home	Home (Executive Dashboard)	1
Setup	Companies	3, 4
	Fiscal Year	5
	Voucher Types	7, 8
	Application Segments	19, 20
	User Groups	21

(*continued*)

Table 1-1. (*continued*)

Menu	Application Segment	APEX Page Number
	Users	22, 23
	Cost Centers	13, 14
	Chart of Accounts	15, 16
	Opening Bank Transactions	17
	Accounts for Financial Statements	18
Select	Switch (Company, Year, and Month)	30
Transactions	Vouchers (to record transactions)	42, 43, 44
Utilities	Reconcile Banks	51, 52
	Search Transaction	53
	Copy Chart of Accounts	54
	Budget Allocation	55
	Reset Password	56
Reports	Vouchers	71
	Ledgers	72
	Trial Balance	73
	Bank Reconciliation	74
	Budget	75
	Financial Statements	76–77
	Feedback Report	302
Closing Process	Vouchers Verification	94, 95
	Month Closing	96
	Temporary Year End	93
	Permanent Year End	97
Feedback	Get feedback from users	300

As a taste of what's to come, Figure 1-1 shows a glimpse of the completed application you are about to build.

Figure 1-1. *Application Dashboard*

1.9 Summary

In this chapter, you went through some basic concepts about cloud computing. Besides being introduced to the three most common types of cloud services, you were briefed about public and private clouds. The basic objective of this book is to reveal how Oracle APEX fits into the cloud computing model with respect to business applications.

To achieve this objective, you will create a GL project that will also enhance your development skills. In the next chapter, you will be provided step-by-step instructions to initiate the project, starting with the application navigation.

CHAPTER 2

Application Navigation

Previous versions of APEX used tabs that acted as an application's main menu up to version 4.2. In APEX 18.1, a default navigation list named the desktop navigation menu is created automatically as a shared component for each new application. This provides the user with a hierarchical set of pull-down menus and submenus. It is displayed as a responsive sidebar. Based on the available space, the navigation bar either displays as a full menu or collapses to a narrow icon bar.

2.1 Create the Main Application Menu

The default desktop navigation menu carries just one item (Home). In this chapter, you'll modify this list to add more application menu entries. Follow these instructions to complete this exercise:

1. In Shared Components, click the Lists option in the Navigation section.

2. Select the Desktop Navigation Menu option, which carries a default entry (Home) created by the application builder wizard. Modify this entry by clicking its name. In the attributes page of the Home menu item, click the pop-up LOV icon to the right of the Image/Class attribute to display a list of possible icon images for the Home menu option. At the top of the icon list you will notice two options: Show and Category; set Show to Font Awesome Icons, and set Category to Web Application. Click the Go button to refresh the view and then select the fa-home icon from the icons list. This image will be displayed for the Home menu at run time. Hit the Apply Changes button to save your work. With practice you

© Riaz Ahmed 2019
R. Ahmed, *Cloud Computing Using Oracle Application Express*,
https://doi.org/10.1007/978-1-4842-4243-8_2

will get to know the icon names and can type them directly in the Image/Class attribute to save time. If you do not see the specified icon, select anyone you like from the list.

3. Click the Create List Entry button to create a new menu item. Enter the values shown in Table 2-1 against the specified attributes. You won't select anything for the first attribute (Parent List Entry) because initially you will create Level 1 entries that do not have parent entries. The target is either a page in the current application or any valid URL. In this case, the Setup menu entry itself is not associated with any application page, so its Target Type is set to No Target.

Table 2-1. *Create First Level 1 Menu Item*

Attribute	Value
Parent List Entry	No Parent List Item
Image/Class	fa-database
List Entry Label	Setup
Target Type	No Target

4. Using the button Create and Create Another, save the previous entry and create five more Level 1 entries, as shown in Table 2-2. Combined, the Target Type and Page attributes inform APEX where to land when a menu item is clicked.

Table 2-2. *Create More Level 1 Menu Items*

Parent List Entry	Image/Class	List Entry Label	Target Type	Page
No Parent List Item	fa-list-alt	Select	Page in this Application	30
No Parent List Item	fa-table	Transactions	Page in this Application	42
No Parent List Item	fa-gear	Utilities	No Target	
No Parent List Item	fa-file-pdf-o	Reports	No Target	
No Parent List Item	fa-calendar	Closing	No Target	

Tables 2-1 and 2-2 show how to construct the main menu of your application. Again, for each of these, you set Parent List Entry to No Parent List Item. Note that the Setup, Utilities, Reports, and Closing entries have no target because these entries are not directly linked to application pages; they link to submenus. In the next step, you will create the submenus for these main entries.

5. Create Level 2 menu entries using Tables 2-3 to 2-6. These entries will appear under their respective main menus (specified under the Parent List Entry column).

Table 2-3. *Setup Menu*

Parent List Entry	Image/Class	List Entry Label	Target Type	Page
Setup	fa-building	Company	Page in this Application	3
Setup	fa-calendar-o	Fiscal Year	Page in this Application	5
Setup	fa-money	Voucher Types	Page in this Application	7
Setup	fa-sitemap	Application Segments	Page in this Application	19
Setup	fa-users	Groups	Page in this Application	21
Setup	fa-user	Users	Page in this Application	22
Setup	fa-tasks	Cost Centers	Page in this Application	13
Setup	fa-newspaper-o	Chart of Accounts	Page in this Application	15
Setup	fa-bank	Opening Bank Transactions	Page in this Application	17
Setup	fa-bar-chart	Financial Statements	Page in this Application	18

Table 2-4. *Utilities Menu*

Parent List Entry	Image/Class	List Entry Label	Target Type	Page
Utilities	fa-bank	Bank Reconciliation	Page in this Application	51
Utilities	fa-search	Search Transaction	Page in this Application	53
Utilities	fa-cc	Copy Chart of Accounts	Page in this Application	54
Utilities	fa-calculator	Budget Allocation	Page in this Application	55
Utilities	fa-ellipsis-h	Reset Password	Page in this Application	56

Table 2-5. *Reports Menu*

Parent List Entry	Image/Class	List Entry Label	Target Type	Page
Reports	fa-money	Vouchers	Page in this Application	71
Reports	fa-book	Ledgers	Page in this Application	72
Reports	fa-reorder	Trial Balance	Page in this Application	73
Reports	fa-bank	Bank Reconciliation	Page in this Application	74
Reports	fa-calculator	Budget	Page in this Application	75
Reports	fa-bar-chart	Financial Statements	Page in this Application	76
Reports	fa-comments	Feedback	Page in this Application	77

Table 2-6. *Closing Menu*

Parent List Entry	Image/Class	List Entry Label	Target Type	Page
Closing	fa-money	Vouchers Verification	Page in this Application	94
Closing	fa-close	Month Closing	Page in this Application	96
Closing	fa-calendar	Temporary Year End	Page in this Application	93
Closing	fa-calendar-o	Permanent Year End	Page in this Application	97

2.2 Modify/Add Navigation Bar Entries

Having created the menus, the final task in this chapter is to design the Navigation Bar. Go to Shared Components, select the Lists option, and then click Desktop Navigation Bar. This will bring up the default navigation bar carrying the default Logout entry. Click the Create List Entry button to add some more entries by using the settings listed in Table 2-7. By defining a parent entry, the Sign Out entry appears as a submenu item. APP_USER and LOGOUT_URL are built-in substitution strings. APP_USER is the current user running the application, while LOGOUT_URL is an application-level attribute used to identify the logout URL. This is a URL that navigates the user to a logout page or optionally directly logs out a user.

Table 2-7. *Navigation Bar Entries*

Attribute	New Entry	New Entry
Parent List Entry	No Parent List Item	No Parent List Item
Image/Class	fa-comments	fa-user
List Entry Label	Feedback	&APP_USER.
Target Type	Page in this Application	No Target
Page	300	
Clear Cache	300	

Figure 2-1 illustrates the navigation menu and navigation bar of your application.

Figure 2-1. *Navigation menu and navigation bar*

15

2.3 Summary

This completes the creation of the menus and navigation bar. In subsequent chapters, you will create the application pages that these menu items will connect to. The next chapter describes the creation of the Company Setup page.

CHAPTER 3

Companies

Let's begin the application-building process by creating the Company Setup, which is very simple. Note that the Home page of your application will contain an executive dashboard that displays various charts based on existing data. Since you do not have any transaction data so far in your database, the Home page will be dealt with in Chapter 29. The Cloud Accountant is capable of handling accounts of multiple companies simultaneously, which is why you have to develop this setup. Each company created through this setup will have a unique code. This code will be saved with every transaction to distinguish one company's data from that of the others.

3.1 Create Application Tables

Because of the referential integrity constraints used in the tables of this application, I recommend you create all the tables at once using the `script.sql` file provided in the book code. Go to SQL Workshop ➤ SQL Scripts ➤ Upload. Click the Browse button, select the `script.sql` file, and click the Upload button. In the SQL Scripts interface, click the Run button ⊙ to execute the script file. On the Run Script page, click the button labeled Run Now. After successfully executing the script file, go to SQL Workshop ➤ Object Browser and verify the objects.

COMPANIES TABLE AND SEQUENCE

```
CREATE TABLE GL_Company
(Cocode NUMBER, Coname VARCHAR2(50), Coaddress VARCHAR2(100), Cophone
VARCHAR2(15), Cofax VARCHAR2(15), Cocity VARCHAR2(15), Cozip VARCHAR2(15),
Cocurrency VARCHAR2(15), CONSTRAINT gl_company_pk PRIMARY KEY (Cocode) ENABLE)

CREATE SEQUENCE gl_company_seq
```

© Riaz Ahmed 2019
R. Ahmed, *Cloud Computing Using Oracle Application Express*,
https://doi.org/10.1007/978-1-4842-4243-8_3

Note   Do not re-execute the CREATE statements because you have already created the objects. These statements will be provided at the top of each chapter just for information.

3.2 Create Pages for Company Setup

Use Table 3-1 to create two pages for this setup. On the first wizard page, select Form, and on the next page, select Report with Form on Table.

Table 3-1. *Attributes for Two Pages*

Page Type	Attribute	Value
Report Page	Page Number	3
	Page Name	Company Setup
	Table/View Name	GL_COMPANY
	Navigation Preference	Identify an existing navigation menu entry for this page.
	Existing Navigation Menu Entry	Setup
Form Page	Page Number	4
Page	Page Name	Company Setup
	Page Mode	Modal Dialog
	Primary Key Type	Select Primary Key Column(s)
	Primary Key Column 1	COCODE
	Source for Primary Key Column 1	Existing Sequence
	Sequence	GL_COMPANY_SEQ
	Form Columns	Select all columns

Note   It is assumed that you have knowledge about all APEX attributes used throughout this book. However, if you are not familiar with any attribute, then click on it in the Properties pane and select the Help tab to see its details.

After creation, modify both pages to set appropriate column headings/labels, as shown in Figure 3-1. Run this segment from the Setup ➤ Companies menu and create at least two companies, also shown in Figure 3-1. That's it!

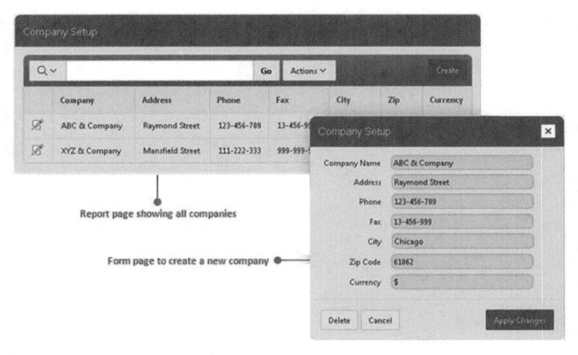

Figure 3-1. *Creating two companies*

3.3 Summary

In this chapter, you created the simplest setup of your application. The next task in the setup hierarchy is to create financial calendars for these established companies.

CHAPTER 4

Fiscal Year

Organizations are required by law to produce a set of annual accounts. To this end, their general ledger systems must maintain a fiscal calendar. Although the specific start and end dates of a fiscal year vary from country to country, for our purposes, the year will start on July 1st and end on June 30th. In addition, each fiscal year is normally subdivided into periods. For our purposes, each period will be a calendar month.

FISCAL YEAR TABLE

```
CREATE TABLE gl_fiscal_year
(Cocode NUMBER Constraint fk_fiscal_year References gl_company (Cocode),
Coyear NUMBER(4), Comonthid NUMBER(2), Comonthname VARCHAR2(9), Pfrom DATE,
Pto DATE, Initial_Year NUMBER(1), Year_Closed NUMBER(1),
Month_Closed NUMBER(1), TYE_Executed DATE,
CONSTRAINT gl_fiscal_year_pk PRIMARY KEY (Cocode,Coyear,Comonthid) ENABLE)
```

This setup will use the previous table. Each company's fiscal year will be distinguished by the company code (cocode), which references its parent key in the Company table. Coyear is a numeric field that will store the year, such as 2015. Comonthid is also a numeric column, and it will hold the ID of each month—in other words, from 1 to 12. The first month—in our case, July—will be marked as 1. Comonthname will store the name of the month, such as September. The two columns, Pfrom and Pto, will store start and end dates for a month, such as 01-JAN-2015 and 31-JAN-2015. A value of 1 in the Initial_Year column signifies that this is the first year of a company; autogeneration of subsequent years will be relative to this initial year. The Year_Closed column tags a year as either open or closed. You'll use this column in the year-end processes in Chapter 24. Month_Closed is used to indicate that a month is closed to further transactions. The TYE_Executed column stores a date value to record when the temporary year end process was last executed. Finally, a table-level primary key constraint is defined, comprising three columns, to prevent duplicate values.

© Riaz Ahmed 2019
R. Ahmed, *Cloud Computing Using Oracle Application Express*,
https://doi.org/10.1007/978-1-4842-4243-8_4

4.1 Create List of Values

The next task is to create two lists of values (LOVs) from scratch. These LOVs will be used to populate the company and month drop-down lists shown in Figure 4-2 later in this chapter. The query defined in the first LOV displays the names of companies in a select list. The code of the selected company is returned and stored in the corresponding page item (P5_COMPANIES) for further processing. The second LOV returns a static numeric value, which will be used to evaluate the first month of the new fiscal year.

Here is LOV 1:

Attribute	Value
Name	Companies
Type	Dynamic
Query	SELECT coname d, cocode r FROM gl_company ORDER BY 1

Here is LOV 2:

Attribute	Value	
Name	Months	
Type	Static	
Display & Return Values	**Display Value**	**Return Value**
	January	1
	February	2
	March	3
	April	4
	May	5
	June	6
	July	7
	August	8
	September	9
	October	10
	November	11
	December	12

4.2 Create Page and Parameters Region

Create a blank page, add the components specified in Table 4-1 onto it, and set their relevant attribute values.

Note   Tables similar to the following are used throughout this book to set up and manipulate the application's pages. The Action column displays the action to be taken. For example, the Create Blank Page entry specifies that a blank page is to be created. The Attribute column identifies the attribute for the Blank Page, while the Value column lists the value of each attribute.

Table 4-1. *Component Values*

Action	Attribute	Value
Create Blank Page	Page Number	5
	Name	Fiscal Year Setup
	Page Mode	Normal
	Breadcrumb	—Don't use breadcrumbs on page—
	Navigation Preference	Identify an existing navigation menu entry for this page
	Existing Navigation Menu Entry	Setup
Create Region	Title	Parameters
	Type	Static Content
	Template	Standard

(*continued*)

Table 4-1. (*continued*)

Action	Attribute	Value
Create Page Item	Name	P5_COMPANIES
	Type	Select List
	Label	Companies
	Region	Parameters
	Start New Row	Yes
	Column and Column Span	Automatic
	Label Column Span	2
	Template	Required
	Value Required	Yes
	LOV Type	Shared Component
	List of Values	COMPANIES
	Display Null Value	Yes
Create Page Item	Name	P5_YEAR
	Type	Text Field
	Label	Year
	Region	Parameters
	Start New Row	No
	Column	Automatic
	New Column	Yes
	Column Span	Automatic
	Label Column Span	2
	Template	Required
	Width	4
	Value Required	Yes
	Maximum Length	4

(*continued*)

Table 4-1. (*continued*)

Action	Attribute	Value
Create Page Item	Name	P5_MONTH
	Type	Select List
	Label	Month
	Region	Parameters
	Start New Row	No
	Column	Automatic
	New Column	Yes
	Column Span	Automatic
	Label Column Span	2
	Template	Required
	Value Required	No
	LOV Type	Shared Component
	List of Values	MONTHS
	Display Null Value	Yes

4.3 Create a Fiscal Year Grid

Next you'll create four regions and a hidden item. The first region (Fiscal Year Setup) is the main region that contains three child regions. It also carries a hidden item (P5_ INITIAL_YEAR) to store the value of the Initial_Year column. This value is used in some processes to evaluate the existence of the selected company's fiscal year. The first child region will display the month names, while the other two will show start and end dates for each month. Use Table 4-2 to create these regions, starting with the main region, which is Fiscal Year Setup.

Table 4-2. *Region Values*

Action	Attribute	Value
Create Region	Title	Fiscal Year Setup
	Type	Static Content
	Template	Standard
Create Region	Title	Month
	Type	Static Content
	Parent Region	**Fiscal Year Setup**
	Template	Standard
	Start New Row	Yes
	Column	Automatic
	Column Span	4 *(Uses Columns 1–4)*
Create Region	Title	From
	Type	Static Content
	Parent Region	**Fiscal Year Setup**
	Template	Standard
	Start New Row	No
	Column	5
	Column Span	2 *(Uses Columns 5 and 6)*
Create Region	Title	To
	Type	Static Content
	Parent Region	**Fiscal Year Setup**
	Template	Standard
	Start New Row	No
	Column	7
	Column Span	2 *(Uses Columns 7 and 8)*

(continued)

Table 4-2. *(continued)*

Action	Attribute	Value
Create Page Item	Name	P5_INITIAL_YEAR
	Type	Hidden
	Value Protected	No
	Region	Fiscal Year Setup

Let's spend a moment reviewing the purpose of what you have done so far. To create a fiscal year, you first select a company from the provided list and then manually enter its initial year before choosing the fiscal year's starting month. All of this will be done in the Parameters region. Then, you'll click a button that will execute a process. The process will generate a fiscal year based on the year and month selections. Thereafter, the generated fiscal year will be displayed in additional page items, which you'll create next.

4.4 Add Items to Hold Months/Dates

Now you must add 12 items to each of the three child regions, as listed in Table 4-3. These items will hold month names and the respective first and last dates for each month.

Table 4-3. *Item Values*

Action	Attribute	Value
Create 12 Page Items	Name	P5_MONTH1, P5_MONTH2, ... P5_ MONTH12
	Type	Display Only
	Label	1., 2., ... 12.
	Save Session State	No
	Region	Month
	Template	Optional

(continued)

Table 4-3. (*continued*)

Action	Attribute	Value
Create 12 Page Items	Name	P5_FROM1, P5_FROM2, ... P5_FROM12
	Type	Display Only
	Label	*Clear Label*
	Save Session State	No
	Region	From
	Template	Optional
Create 12 Page Items	Name	P5_TO1, P5_TO2, ... P5_TO12
	Type	Display Only
	Label	*Clear Label*
	Save Session State	No
	Region	To
	Template	Optional

4.5 Create Buttons to Generate, Save, and Remove a Fiscal Year

In this section, using Table 4-4, you will add three buttons to the Fiscal Year Setup region to generate, save, and delete a fiscal year. You use JavaScript behind the Delete button to present the delete confirmation box.

Table 4-4. *Button Values*

Action	Attribute	Value
Create Button	Button Name	Generate
	Label	Generate Fiscal Year
	Region	Fiscal Year Setup
	Button Position	Copy
	Hot	Yes
	Action	Submit Page
Create Button	Button Name	Save
	Label	Save
	Region	Fiscal Year Setup
	Button Position	Copy
	Hot	No
	Action	Submit Page
Create Button	Button Name	**Delete**
	Label	Delete
	Region	Fiscal Year Setup
	Button Position	Copy
	Hot	No
	Action	Redirect to URL
	URL Target	javascript:apex.confirm('Delete Fiscal Year?', '**Delete**');
	Execute Validations	Yes (*associated with "4.10 Create Validation: Check Transaction"*)

Note   The Delete request defined in JavaScript is case-sensitive and must match the value specified in the Button Name attribute.

In the next section, you'll create the processes that will run each time a button is clicked.

4.6 Generate Fiscal Year Process

After creating a new company, you select the company along with its starting fiscal year and month. You then click the Generate button on the page, which automatically generates a complete fiscal year for the company. This automatic generation of the fiscal year is backed by the first of the processes that you are going to add in this section. On the Fiscal Year Setup page, click the Processing tab. Then right-click the Processing node and select Create Process from the menu. Set the attributes defined in Table 4-5 for this process. You will find the PL/SQL code for this chapter in the Chapter4 folder.

Table 4-5. *Process Attributes*

Action	Attribute	Value
Create Process	Name	Generate Fiscal Year
	Type	PL/SQL Code
	PL/SQL Code	Book_Code\Chapter4\Generate Fiscal Year.txt
	Point	Processing
	When Button Pressed	Generate

In this PL/SQL block, the financial year runs only from July to June; therefore, no calendar will be generated if the selected month is something other than July. You may enhance the code if you want to add other fiscal year combinations. I incremented the year value in December to show the correct year for the months of January to June. I also made a provision for leap years in February.

4.7 Save Fiscal Year Process

After generating a fiscal year on the screen, you'll click the Save button, which invokes the process defined in Table 4-6. The process comprises 12 simple insert statements. It collects values from the page items and inserts them into the GL_FISCAL_YEAR table. Note that this process and the one that follows will be created under the Generate Fiscal Year process.

Table 4-6. *Save Process*

Action	Attribute	Value
Create Process	Name	Save Fiscal Year
	Type	PL/SQL Code
	PL/SQL Code	Book_Code\Chapter4\Save Fiscal Year.txt
	Point	Processing
	Success Message	Fiscal Year Saved successfully
	When Button Pressed	Save

4.8 Delete Fiscal Year Process

You can also remove erroneously created fiscal years using the process mentioned in Table 4-7 that runs when the delete button is clicked. A year can be deleted only when it passes the Check Transaction validation (see Table 4-9).

Table 4-7. *Delete Process*

Action	Attribute	Value
Create Process	Name	Delete Fiscal Year
	Type	PL/SQL Code
	PL/SQL Code	DELETE FROM gl_fiscal_year WHERE cocode=:P5_COMPANIES AND coyear=:P5_YEAR;
	Point	Processing
	Success Message	Fiscal year deleted successfully
	When Button Pressed	Delete

4.9 Fetch Fiscal Year Dynamic Action

As the name implies, this dynamic action will fetch the initial fiscal year of a company from the database when you select a company from the P5_COMPANIES select list. Click the Dynamic Actions tab, right-click the Change node, and select Create Dynamic Action from the context menu. Set the attributes mentioned in Table 4-8 for the new dynamic action.

Table 4-8. *Action Attributes*

Action	Attribute	Value
Create Dynamic Action	Name	Fetch Fiscal Year
	Event	Change
	Selection Type	Item(s)
	Item(s)	P5_COMPANIES
	Action (under the Show node)	Execute PL/SQL Code
	PL/SQL Code	Book_Code\Chapter4\Fetch Fiscal Year. txt
	Page Items to Submit	P5_COMPANIES
	Page Items to Return	The Fetch Fiscal Year process will retrieve fiscal year values from the database and will return these to the items specified in the Page items to Return attribute. Because it's a long list comprising almost all page items, I created a separate text file for your convenience: Book_Code\Chapter4\ Page Items to Return.txt
	Fire on Initialization	No

4.10 Create Validation: Check Transaction

The following validation will check for the existence of data before the deletion of a fiscal year. The delete request will be refused if any record exists in the transactions table. Go to the Processing tab, right-click the Validating node, and select Create Validation. Set the attributes mentioned in Table 4-9 for this validation.

Table 4-9. *Validation Attributes*

Action	Attribute	Value
Create Validation	Name	Check Transaction
	Type	PL/SQL Function Body (returning Boolean)
	PL/SQL Function Body (returning Boolean)	Book_Code\Chapter4\Check Transaction.txt
	Error Message	Can't delete; transactions exist in this year
	When Button Pressed	Delete

4.11 Create Branch

After deleting a fiscal year, you need to clear the cache. The following branch performs this process. In the Processing tab, right-click the After Processing node, and select Create Branch. Set the attributes mentioned in Table 4-10 for this branch.

Table 4-10. *Branch Attributes*

Action	Attribute	Value
Create Branch	Name	Clear Cache
	Point	After Processing
	Behavior Type	Page or URL (redirect)
	Target Type	Page in this Application
	Page	5
	Clear Cache	5
	When Button Pressed	Delete

4.12 Dynamic Actions to Hide Buttons

After creating a fiscal year, you must hide the Save and Generate buttons and show the Delete button. Similarly, you must hide the Delete button and show the other two when a new fiscal year is being generated. Create the dynamic actions (using Tables 4-11 to 4-19) to achieve these tasks. These dynamic actions will run when a fiscal year for the selected company exists—in other words, when the value of the hidden item P5_INITIAL_YEAR equals 1. Note that this value is retrieved from the database through Fetch Fiscal Year dynamic action, as shown earlier in Table 4-8.

First, you hide the Save button (see Table 4-11).

Table 4-11. *Action: Hide Save Button*

Action	Attribute	Value
Create Dynamic Action	Name	Hide Save Button
	Event	Change
	Selection Type	Item(s)
	Item	P5_INITIAL_YEAR
Client-side Condition	Type	Item=Value
	Item	P5_INITIAL_YEAR
	Value	1

Click the Show node under the True node to set the attributes in Table 4-12. These attributes will hide the Save button when the value of P5_INITIAL_YEAR is equal to 1.

Table 4-12. *Action: Hide*

Attribute	Value
Action *(Under Show node)*	Hide
Selection Type	Button
Button	Save

Now, right-click the False node, and select Create False Action. A new node (Show) will be added, as shown in Figure 4-1.

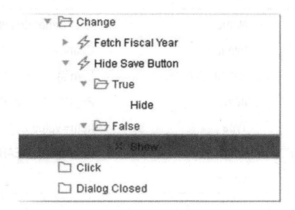

Figure 4-1. *The new node*

Set the attributes in Table 4-13 for the false action to show the Save button when the value of P5_INITIAL_YEAR is NOT equal to 1.

Table 4-13. *Action: Show*

Attribute	Value
Action	Show
Selection Type	Button
Button	Save

Next you create a dynamic action to hide/show the Generate button (see Table 4-14).

Table 4-14. *Action: Hide Generate Fiscal Year Button*

Action	Attribute	Value
Create Dynamic Action	Name	Hide Generate Fiscal Year Button
	Event	Change
	Selection Type	Item(s)
	Item	P5_INITIAL_YEAR
Client-Side Condition	Type	Item=Value
	Item	P5_INITIAL_YEAR
	Value	1

Table 4-15 shows the true action attributes.

Table 4-15. *True Action Attributes*

Attribute	Value
Action	Hide
Selection Type	Button
Button	Generate

Table 4-16 shows the false action attributes.

Table 4-16. *False Action Attributes*

Attribute	Value
Action	Show
Selection Type	Button
Button	Generate

Finally, create one more dynamic action to hide/show the Delete button, as shown in Table 4-17.

Table 4-17. *Action: Show Delete Button*

Action	Attribute	Value
Create Dynamic Action	Name	Show Delete Button
	Event	Change
	Selection Type	Item(s)
	Item	P5_INITIAL_YEAR
Client-Side Condition	Type	Item=Value
	Item	P5_INITIAL_YEAR
	Value	1

Table 4-18 shows the true action attributes.

Table 4-18. *Show Attributes*

Attribute	Value
Action	Show
Selection Type	Button
Button	Delete

Table 4-19 lists the false action attributes.

Table 4-19. *Hide Attributes*

Attribute	Value
Action	Hide
Selection Type	Button
Button	Delete

4.13 Test Your Work

Save the page and run it from the Setup ➤ Fiscal Year menu. It should look similar to Figure 4-2. Follow these instructions to create a fiscal year for ABC & Company:

1. Select ABC & Company from the Companies select list.

2. Enter **2015** in the Year box.

3. Select July from the Month select list.

4. Hit the Generate Fiscal Year button. This should display a fiscal year starting from 01-JUL-2015 to 30-JUN-2016. Since 2016 is a leap year, the process adds an extra day onto the month of February.

5. Click the Save button.

6. Repeat Steps 2 through 5 to generate a calendar for the other company.

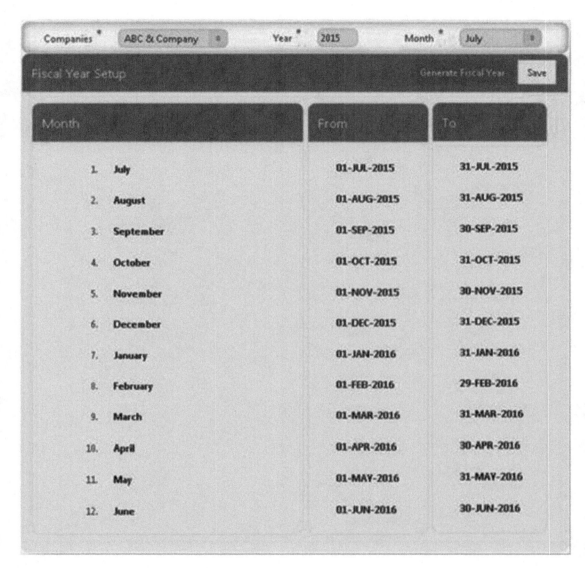

Figure 4-2. *Creating a fiscal year*

4.14 Summary

In this chapter, you generated fiscal years for the two companies you created in the previous chapter. Each fiscal year comprises 12 periods, and every transaction you create in the application will be posted in one of these periods. In the next chapter, you will create another application segment called Voucher Types.

CHAPTER 5

Voucher Types

Financial transactions are recorded in ledgers using special forms called *vouchers*. Before creating the actual interface for vouchers, you are going to create a Setup page to define different voucher types. Vouchers are broadly divided into three categories: payment, receipt, and journal. Each one has its own specific interface to record transactions.

However, in this book, you will create a single interface for all three. By creating this setup, you'll allow the end users to create custom voucher types to distinguish between transactions. Creating this setup is similar to the Company setup described previously. The only difference is the use of Radio Group items that will identify the nature of a voucher type. The database table GL_VOUCHER contains a column named VCHNATURE. This column holds information about the nature of the vouchers. For example, payment vouchers will be flagged as type 1, receipt vouchers will be marked as type 2, and journal vouchers will be identified as type 3. You will also create a sequence to autogenerate primary key values for the table.

VOUCHER TYPES TABLE AND SEQUENCE

```
CREATE TABLE gl_voucher
(Vchcode NUMBER, Vchtype VARCHAR2(6), Vchtitle VARCHAR2(30), Vchnature
NUMBER(1),
 CONSTRAINT GL_VOUCHER_PK PRIMARY KEY (Vchcode) ENABLE)

CREATE SEQUENCE gl_voucher_seq
```

5.1 Create List of Values

Create a list of values (LOV) from scratch. This LOV will be linked to the voucher nature radio item. Set the Name attribute of this LOV to Voucher Nature, and set Type to Static. Set Display and Return values, as defined in Table 5-1.

© Riaz Ahmed 2019
R. Ahmed, *Cloud Computing Using Oracle Application Express*,
https://doi.org/10.1007/978-1-4842-4243-8_5

Table 5-1. *Voucher Nature List of Values*

Display Value	Return Value
PV	1
RV	2
JV	3

5.2 Create Pages for Voucher Types Setup

Create a new page by selecting the Form and Report with Form on Table options in the page creation wizard. Set the attributes for the two pages as shown in Table 5-2.

Table 5-2. *Page Attributes*

Page Type	Attribute	Value
Report Page	Page Number	7
	Page Name	Voucher Types Report
	Table/View Name	GL_VOUCHER
	Navigation Preference	Identify an existing navigation menu entry for this page.
	Existing Navigation Menu Entry	Setup
	Report Columns	*Select all the columns to include in the report page.*
Form Page	Page Number	8
	Page Name	Voucher Types Form
	Page Mode	Modal Dialog
	Primary Key Type	Select Primary Key Column(s)
	Primary Key Column 1	VCHCODE
	Source for Primary Key Column 1	Existing Sequence
	Sequence	GL_VOUCHER_SEQ
	Form Columns	*Select all the columns to include in the form page.*

After creation, modify the attributes of page 8 so they match Table 5-3.

Table 5-3. *Page 8 Attributes*

Action	Attribute	Value
Modify Page Items	Name	P8_VCHTYPE
	Label	Type
	Template	Required
	Value Required	Yes
	Name	P8_VCHTITLE
	Label	Title
	Template	Required
	Value Required	Yes

5.2.1 Convert Text Item to Radio Group

The final task of this setup is to convert the page item representing the VCHNATURE column from a text item to a radio group. Click the P8_VCHNATURE page item, and set the attributes defined in Table 5-4.

Table 5-4. *VCHNATURE Attributes*

Attribute	Value
Type	Radio Group
Label	Nature
Number of Columns	3
Template	Required
Value Required	Yes
LOV Type	Shared Component
List of Values	VOUCHER NATURE
Display Extra Value	No
Display Null Value	No
Default Type	Static Value
Static Value	3 (i.e., JV)

5.3 Create Validation: Check Transaction

Create a validation to prevent the deletion of voucher types with generated transactions. Select the Processing tab, right-click the Validating node, and then click the Create Validation option in the context menu. Now set the attributes of this validation, as mentioned in Table 5-5.

Table 5-5. *Validation Attributes*

Action	Attribute	Value
Create Validation	Name	Check Transaction
	Type	PL/SQL Function Body (returning Boolean)
	PL/SQL Function Body Returning Boolean	Book_Code\Chapter5\Check Transaction.txt
	Error Message	Can't delete voucher type with generated transactions
	When Button Pressed	DELETE

5.4 Test Your Work

Add the appropriate labels for the columns on both forms, as shown in Figure 5-1. Save the page and run this feature from the Setup | Voucher Types menu. Create the three voucher types, as illustrated in the title picture. Voucher types having cash or a bank involved must be of a payment (PV) or receipt (RV) nature; all other types can be assigned to the journal (JV) nature.

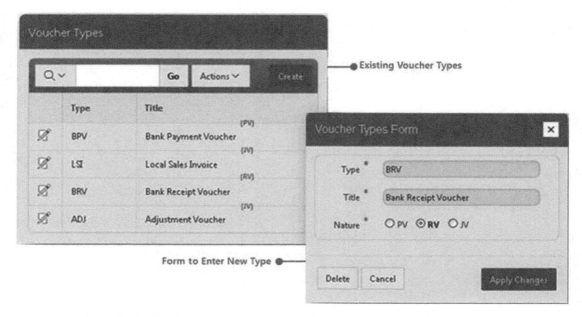

Figure 5-1. *Labels for the columns on both forms*

5.5 Summary

By adding this setup, you allow users to create custom voucher types to distinguish financial transactions according to their nature. The GL application consists of various segments that will be used in a multiuser environment. To control user access to these segments, you will create a strong security module. But first you have to identify and store those segments in the database, which is the topic of the next chapter.

CHAPTER 6

Application Segments

In this chapter, you will create a setup that provides a list of all the different parts of the application. Just like a site map created for websites, it is displayed as a tree view of the application and is created to implement application security. There are three main components in the application to which you should apply security: menus (including the main and submenus), pages, and items (such as buttons). The fourth one (app) is called the root node and is used to distinguish between segments of multiple applications.

After creating all the application segments here, you will use them in the next chapter to enforce application access rules. It's a flexible module, which is designed in such a way as to accommodate future application enhancements.

SEGMENTS TABLE AND SEQUENCE

```
CREATE TABLE gl_segments
(segmentID NUMBER, segmentTitle VARCHAR2(50), segmentParent NUMBER,
segmentType VARCHAR2(4),
pageID NUMBER(4), itemRole VARCHAR2(10), CONSTRAINT gl_segments_pk PRIMARY
KEY (segmentID) ENABLE)

CREATE SEQUENCE gl_segments_seq MINVALUE 1 START WITH 1 INCREMENT
BY 1 CACHE 20
```

Each application segment will be stored in this table with a unique ID (segmentID). To present these segments in a hierarchal format, the segmentParent column will store the ID of each segment's parent. Each entry in this table will have a type that will be stored in the segmentType column. The pageID column will be stored with each segment to identify its location. The itemRole column specifies the role of page items (buttons and select lists). For example, the create button on a page performs the role of record creation, so the Create role will be assigned to this button.

© Riaz Ahmed 2019
R. Ahmed, *Cloud Computing Using Oracle Application Express*,
https://doi.org/10.1007/978-1-4842-4243-8_6

6.1 Create Lists of Values

Create two static lists of values (LOVs) from scratch using Tables 6-1 and 6-2. The values included in these LOVs will be utilized in the segment creation form to identify the type of segments and the roles performed by page items.

Table 6-1. *LOV Name: Segment Type*

Display Value	Return Value
App	App
Item	Item
Menu	Menu
Page	Page

Table 6-2. *LOV Name: Item Role*

Display Value	Return Value
Create	Create
Modify	Modify
Delete	Delete
Save	Save
Print	Print
Display	Display

6.2 Create Segments Setup Pages

Use Table 6-3 to create two pages. On the first wizard page, select the Form option followed by Report with Form on Table.

Table 6-3. *Segments Setup Pages*

Page Type	Attribute	Value
Report Page	Page Number	19
	Page Name	Application Segments Report
	Table/View Name	GL_SEGMENTS
	Navigation Preference	Identify an existing navigation menu entry for this page.
	Existing Navigation Menu Entry	Setup
	Report Columns	*Select all the columns to include in the report page.*
Form Page	Page Number	20
	Page Name	Application Segments Form
	Page Mode	Modal Dialog
	Primary Key Type	Select Primary Key Column(s)
	Primary Key Column 1	SEGMENTID
	Source for Primary Key Column 1	Existing Sequence
	Sequence	GL_SEGMENTS_SEQ
	Form Columns	*Select all the columns to include in the form page.*

After creation, modify the form page (page 20) to change the item labels, as shown in Figure 6-1.

6.3 Modify Segments Form

Amend the Application Segments Form's items as indicated in Table 6-4. The P20_ SEGMENTPARENT item is being transformed into a pop-up LOV. It will display title and type columns from the segments table to allow the selection of a parent for a new entry. Since the Item segment type doesn't have any children, the LOV will exclude these records.

Table 6-4. *Application Segments Form Attributes*

Action	Attribute	Value
Modify Items	Names	P20_SEGMENTTITLE, P20_SEGMENTPARENT & P20_SEGMENTTYPE
	Template	Required
	Value Required	Yes
Modify Item	Name	P20_SEGMENTPARENT
	Type	Pop-up LOV
	Type (LOV)	SQL Query
	SQL Query	SELECT segmentTitleǁ' ('ǁsegmentTypeǁ')' d, segmentID r FROM gl_segments WHERE segmentType != '**Item**' ORDER BY pageID,segmentID,segmentParent
	Default Type	Static Value
	Static Value	0
Modify Item	Name	P20_SEGMENTTYPE
	Type	Select List
	LOV Type	Shared Component
	LOV	SEGMENT TYPE
Modify Item	Name	P20_PAGEID
	Template	Optional
	Width	4
	Maximum Length	4
Modify Item	Name	P20_ITEMROLE
	Type	Select List
	Template	Optional
	LOV Type	Shared Component
	LOV	ITEM ROLE

6.4 Add Tree View Region

Currently, the report page (19) contains an interactive report region to display all segments in a matrix report. In this section, you will change this appearance to display all the segments in a tree view, as shown in Figure 6-1. First, delete the existing Application Segments region from page 19 and then add a new region to this page using the attributes shown in Table 6-5.

Table 6-5. *Tree View Region Attributes*

Attribute	Value
Title	Application Segments
Type	Tree
Type (under Source)	SQL Query
SQL Query	Book_Code\Chapter6\Tree Query.txt
Template	Standard

Click the Attributes node under the Application Segments tree and set the following properties:

Node Label Column	TITLE
Node Value Column	VALUE
Hierarchy	Not Computed
Node Status Column	STATUS
Hierarchy Level Column	LEVEL
Link Column	LINK
Icon CSS Class Column	ICON

6.5 Create Buttons

Right-click the new Application Segments tree region and select Create Button from the context menu. Set the attributes for this button, as shown in Table 6-6. This button will be used to create a new application segment.

Table 6-6. *Create Button Attributes*

Attribute	Value
Button Name	Create
Label	Create
Region	Application Segments
Button Position	Copy
Hot	Yes
Action	Redirect to Page In This Application
Target	Type = Page In This Application Page = 20 Clear Cache = 20

Create another button named Refresh using the attributes indicated in Table 6-7. This button is added to refresh the segments tree.

Table 6-7. *Refresh Button Attributes*

Attribute	Value
Button Name	Refresh
Label	Refresh
Region	Application Segments
Button Position	Copy
Button Template	Text with Icon
Hot	No
Icon	fa-undo
Action	Redirect to Page In This Application
Target	Type = Page In This Application Page = &APP_PAGE_ID.

6.6 Create Validations

Using the Table 6-8, create two validations on page 20 to prevent the deletion of used segments.

Table 6-8. *Validation Attributes*

Action	Attribute	Value
Create Validation	Name	Check Segment
	Type	PL/SQL Function (returning Error Text)
	PL/SQL Function Body Returning Error Text	Book_Code\Chapter6\Check Segment.txt
	When Button Pressed	DELETE
Create Validation	Name	Check Child Segment
	Type	PL/SQL Function (returning Error Text)
	PL/SQL Function Body Returning Error Text	Book_Code\Chapter5\Check Child Segment.txt
	When Button Pressed	DELETE

6.7 Create Branch

After clicking the Create button on the Application Segments form page, you will get a message indicating that your action was processed successfully, but you'll notice that the values still exist on the form. To create uninterrupted records in a blank form, create a branch under the After Processing node and set the attributes specified in Table 6-9.

Table 6-9. *Branch Attributes*

Action	Attribute	Value
Create Branch	Name	Clear Page 20
	Point	After Processing
	Behavior Type	Page or URL (Redirect)
	Target	Type = Page In This Application Page = 20 Clear Cache = 20
	When Button Pressed	CREATE

One more thing that you must do in order to stay on page 20 is to remove the CREATE button value from the request specified in the Close Dialog process. In the Processing tab, click the Close Dialog process. Scroll down to the Condition section in the properties editor, and remove the CREATE entry from the Value list. By default, the modal page is closed when Create, Save, or Delete buttons are clicked. By removing the CREATE entry, the dialog page will be closed only when the Save (labeled Apply Changes) or Delete buttons are clicked. This way you will stay on page 20 to create additional segment records.

6.8 Test Your Work

Everything is set! Now it is the time to test your work. Save your work and run the Application Segments module from the Setup menu. Click the Create button, and enter the records mentioned in Table 6-10, one after the other, in the segments form.

Table 6-10. *List of Application Segments*

	Segment Title	Parent	Type	Page ID	Item Role
1	The Cloud Accountant	0	App		
2	Home Menu	The Cloud Accountant	Menu		
3	Home	Home Menu	Page	1	
4	Select Menu	The Cloud Accountant	Menu		
5	Select (Company/Year/Month)	Select Menu	Page	30	
6	Switch Company	Select (Company/Year/Month)	Item	30	Modify
7	Switch Year	Select (Company/Year/Month)	Item	30	Modify
8	Switch Month	Select (Company/Year/Month)	Item	30	Modify

■ Application   ■ Menu   ■ Page   ■ Item

The first entry in Table 6-10 will create the application root; therefore, no parent is assigned to it. Recall that you assigned the default value (zero) for the parent item in Table 6-4. The second and fourth main menu entries will come under the application root. The first page entry defined in line 3 will be placed under the Home menu, along with the corresponding page number. Similarly, the Select page defined in line 5 will come under the Select menu. The last level of your application hierarchy belongs to page items (lines 6–8). The Select page (30) will have three select lists (Company, Year, and Month), so these items are set under page 30. If you mark the Type of an entry as an Item, then you must also specify its role. Roles will be used in Chapter 31 to implement application security. The list in Table 6-10 is a subset of a comprehensive list that covers all of the application's segments. You can find the complete list in the `application_segments.xlsx` file in the book code's Chapter 6 folder. Open it up and add all application segments to complete this chapter. Note that it is not necessary to follow the defined sequence while creating new segments; you can add an entry to any level, any time. The important thing is to select the correct parent under which to place the new entry. Figure 6-1 provides an overview of the two Application Segments pages.

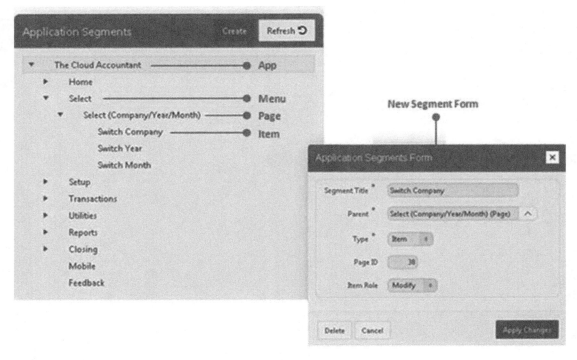

Figure 6-1. *Segments pages*

6.9 Summary

In this chapter, you created a hierarchy of your application segments that will be used to control application access in the next chapter.

CHAPTER 7

User Groups

In the previous chapter, you laid the foundation of your application's security that will be imposed on menus, pages, and page items. In this chapter, you will create user groups. Allocating application rights to individual users is a tedious activity, and it's not recommended because it is highly error-prone. You can create a few user groups and assign application privileges to them instead. Users are created afterward and then associated with their respective groups. This means all users inherit application rights from the group (or groups) to which they belong. For example, to handle application security for a staff of more than 100 employees, comprising managers and data entry clerks, you will create just two groups (managers and clerks) with appropriate privileges. Any changes made to the privileges of these groups will be automatically inherited by all associated users.

USER GROUPS TABLES

```
CREATE TABLE gl_groups_master
(groupID NUMBER(4), groupTitle VARCHAR2(25), CONSTRAINT gl_groups_pk PRIMARY
KEY (groupID) ENABLE)

CREATE TABLE gl_groups_detail
(groupID NUMBER(4) CONSTRAINT fk_Group_Detail REFERENCES gl_groups_
master(groupID), segmentID NUMBER CONSTRAINT fk_user_groups REFERENCES gl_
segments(segmentID), segmentParent NUMBER, segmentType VARCHAR2(4), pageID
NUMBER(4), itemRole VARCHAR2(10), allow_access VARCHAR2(1))
```

In this setup, you will be using two tables. The master table will hold IDs and titles of groups, while the details table will contain all application privileges (specified in the segments setup) for each group.

© Riaz Ahmed 2019
R. Ahmed, *Cloud Computing Using Oracle Application Express*,
https://doi.org/10.1007/978-1-4842-4243-8_7

7.1 Page and Parameters Region

You will set up user groups using just one application page. This page will carry two main regions: Parameters and Group's Privileges. In the Parameters region, you indicate whether you are creating a new group or are manipulating an existing one. Based on this selection, you'll be provided with the appropriate interface. For example, if you're trying to modify or delete an existing group, then you'll select the Existing option, followed by a group from the provided list. When you select the New option, a different interface will be presented to allow you to create a new group. Just like the Financial Year setup, you'll start by creating a blank page for this setup. Use Table 7-1 to add a blank page and other components to the page.

Table 7-1. *Page and Parameters Region Attributes*

Action	Attribute	Value
Create Blank Page	Page Number	21
	Name	User Groups
	Page Mode	Normal
	Breadcrumb	—Do not use breadcrumbs on page—
	Navigation Preference	Identify an existing navigation menu entry for this page.
	Existing Navigation Menu Entry	Setup
Create Region	Title	Parameters
	Type	Static Content
	Template	Standard
Create Page Item	Name	P21_EXISTINGNEW
	Type	Radio Group
	Label	Action:
	Number of Columns	2
	Page Action on Selection	Submit Page (*to show/hide Group's Privileges region*)

(*continued*)

Table 7-1. (*continued*)

Action	Attribute	Value
	Region	Parameters
	Start New Row	Yes
	Column/Column Span	Automatic
	Label Column Span	1
	Template	Required
	Type (LOV)	Static Values
	Static Values	STATIC:New;NEW,Existing;EXISTING
	Display Null Value	No
	Type (Default)	Static Value
	Static Value	EXISTING
Create Page Item	Name	P21_GROUPID1
	Type	Select List
	Label	Group:
	Page Action on Selection	Submit Page (*to refresh Selected Segment region*)
	Region	Parameters
	Start New Row	No
	Column/Column Span	Column=4/Column Span=5
	LOV Type	SQL Query
	SQL Query	SELECT DISTINCT groupTitle d, groupID r FROM gl_groups_master ORDER BY groupID
	Type	Item = Value
	Item	P21_EXISTINGNEW
	Value	EXISTING (*the list is displayed only when EXISTING option is on*)

(*continued*)

Table 7-1. (*continued*)

Action	Attribute	Value
Create Page Item	Name	P21_GROUPTITLE1 (*used in the Tree region's title*)
	Type	Hidden
	Region	Parameters
	Type (Source)	SQL Query (return single value)
	SQL Query	SELECT groupTitle FROM gl_groups_master WHERE groupID=:P21_ GROUPID1
	Source Used	Always, replacing any existing value in session state
Create Page Item	Name	P21_GROUPID2 (*to assign a new ID to a new group*)
	Type	Display Only
	Label	Group ID:
	Region	Parameters
	Start New Row	No
	Column	4
	Column Span	2
	Type (Source)	SQL Query (return single value)
	SQL Query	SELECT MAX(groupID)+1 FROM gl_groups_master
	Source Used	Always, replacing any existing value in session state
	Type (Default)	Static Value
	Static Value	1
	Server-side Condition	Item = Value
	Item	P21_EXISTINGNEW
	Value	NEW

(*continued*)

Table 7-1. (*continued*)

Action	Attribute	Value
Create Page Item	Name	P21_GROUPTITLE2 (*title for a new group*)
	Type	Text Field
	Label	Title:
	Region	Parameters
	Start New Row	No
	Column	Automatic
	New Column	Yes
	Column Span	Automatic
	Server-side Condition	Item = Value
	Item	P21_EXISTINGNEW
	Value	NEW

Note   The two items (P21_GROUPID2 and P21_GROUPTITLE2) are displayed only when the NEW option is on. Make sure that the Value attribute NEW doesn't have any leading or trailing blanks.

7.2 Buttons

Add two buttons to the Parameters region, as mentioned in Table 7-2. These buttons will be displayed on the new group creation form. Clicking the Create Group—Allow All button will create a group with all the application access privileges, while clicking the Create Group—Disallow All button will create a group without any privileges.

Table 7-2. *Button Attributes*

Attribute	Button 1	Button 2
Name	Allow	Disallow
Label	Create Group—Allow All	Create Group—Disallow All
Region	Parameters	Parameters
Button Position	Create	Create
Action	Submit Page	Submit Page
Server-side Condition	Item = Value	Item = Value
Item	P21_EXISTINGNEW	P21_EXISTINGNEW
Value	NEW	NEW

7.3 New Group Process

This process is associated with the two buttons created in the previous section. The condition says that if the request came from any of the two buttons, then execute the PL/SQL process to create the group with all or no privileges. Under the Processing tab, right-click the Processing node and choose Create Process to create a new process, as specified in Table 7-3.

Table 7-3. *New Group Process Attributes*

Action	Attribute	Value
Create Process	Name	Create New Group
	Type	PL/SQL Code
	PL/SQL Code	Book_Code\Chapter7\Create New Group. txt
	Point	Processing
	Success Message	Group Created Successfully
	Error Message	Could not create group
	Server-side Condition	Request is contained in Value
	Value	Allow,Disallow *(Case-Sensitive, should match with the button names provided above)*

7.4 Delete Group Button

Create a button (as mentioned in Table 7-4) to delete an existing group. When you submit the page through this button, the process Delete Group (created next) is executed.

Table 7-4. *Delete Group Button Attributes*

Action	Attribute	Value
Create Button	Name	Delete
	Label	Delete Group
	Region	Parameters
	Button Position	Create
	Hot	Yes
	Action	Submit Page
	Server-side Condition	Item = Value
	Item	P21_EXISTINGNEW
	Value	EXISTING

7.5 Delete Group Process

Create a new process (as specified in Table 7-5) to drop a group. This process will execute only when the user selects a group from the select list—in other words, when the value of the page item P21_GROUPID1 is not zero. Note that the GL_USERS table already has a constraint to avoid the deletion of a group with associated users.

Table 7-5. *Delete Group Process Attributes*

Action	Attribute	Value
Create Process	Name	Delete Group
	Type	PL/SQL Code
	PL/SQL Code	DELETE FROM gl_groups_detail WHERE groupID=:P21_GroupID1; DELETE FROM gl_groups_master WHERE groupID=:P21_GroupID1;
	Point	Processing
	Success Message	Group Deleted Successfully
	Error Message	Could not delete group
	When Button Pressed	Delete
	Server-side Condition	Item is NOT NULL and NOT zero
	Item	P21_GROUPID1

7.6 Group Privileges Region

This is another static content region that will carry tree and classic report regions to display the application access privileges of a selected group. The region will be displayed only when you select the EXISTING option from the radio group. Use Table 7-6 to create this region.

Table 7-6. *Group Privileges Region Attributes*

Action	Attribute	Value
Create Region	Title	Group's Privileges
	Type	Static Content
	Server-side Condition	Item = Value
	Item	P21_EXISTINGNEW
	Value	EXISTING

7.7 Tree Region

Add a tree region to the Group's Privileges region (using Table 7-7) to display the application access rights of the selected group. The query used for this tree is similar to the one used in Chapter 6, except for the link column, which uses the inline JavaScript call `'javascript:pageItemName('||apex_escape.js_literal(segmentid)||')'` As `link` to a function named `pageItemName`, defined in Table 7-7. The `APEX_ESCAPE` package provides functions for escaping special characters in strings to ensure that the data is suitable for further processing. The `JS_LITERAL` function, of the `APEX_ESCAPE` package, escapes and optionally enquotes a JavaScript string. Note: Click the Attributes node under the Group: &P21_GROUPTITLE1. tree and set the properties mentioned after the *Parent Region* attribute.

Table 7-7. *Tree Region Attributes*

Action	Attribute	Value
Create Region	Title	Group: &P21_GROUPTITLE1
	Type	Tree
	Type (under Source)	SQL Query
	SQL Query	Book_Code\Chapter7\Tree Query.txt
	Parent Region	Group's Privileges
	Node Label Column	TITLE
	Node Value Column	VALUE
	Hierarchy	Not Computed
	Node Status Column	STATUS
	Hierarchy Level Column	LEVEL
	Link Column	LINK
	Icon CSS Class Column	ICON
	Select Node Page Item (Under Attributes)	P21_SELECTED_NODE *(to save the Tree state)*

(continued)

Table 7-7 *(continued)*

Action	Attribute	Value
Create Page Item	Name	P21_SELECTED_NODE
	Type	Hidden
	Value Protected	No
	Region	Group: &P21_GROUPTITLE1.
Modify Page 21	Function and Global Variable Declaration *(Click on the root node [Page 21: User Groups] to enter this code)*	function pageItemName(selectedNode) { $s('P21_SELECTED_NODE', selectedNode); }

The function (`pageItemName`) is called in the tree's query link. The calling procedure (in the query) passes a segment ID to the function's `selectedNode` parameter. The `$s` (which is a JavaScript function) sets the value of a hidden page item (P21_SELECTED_NODE) to the value received in the selectedNode parameter, which is then used to refresh another region (Selected Segment) to display the relevant segment along with its access privilege.

7.8 Add Classic Report Region

This report will show the name of the selected segment, along with its access privilege. A button will also be added to this region to allow/revoke the access right. The report is presented using a query that is based on the value of the hidden item, which is P21_SELECTED_NODE. Set the attributes as indicated in Table 7-8 for this region.

Table 7-8. *Classic Report Region Attributes*

Action	Attribute	Value
Create Region	Title	Selected Segment
	Type	Classic Report
	Type (under Source)	SQL Query
	SQL Query	SELECT s.segmentTitle,g.allow_access FROM gl_segments s, gl_groups_detail g WHERE s.segmentID=:P21_SELECTED_NODE AND s.segmentID=g.segmentID AND g.groupID=:P21_GROUPID1
	Page Items to Submit	P21_SELECTED_NODE
	Parent Region	Group's Privileges
	Start New Row	No
	Server-side Condition	Item = Value
	Item	P21_EXISTINGNEW
	Value	EXISTING

7.9 Dynamic Action to Refresh Region

You also need to refresh the classic report region (Selected Segment) with the appropriate data when the user switches from one tree node to another. The dynamic action mentioned in Table 7-9 serves this purpose. Create this dynamic action under the Change node.

Table 7-9. *Dynamic Action to Refresh Region*

Action	Attribute	Value
Create Dynamic Action	Name	Refresh Region
	Event	Change
	Selection Type	Item(s)
	Item(s)	P21_SELECTED_NODE
	Action *(under Show node)*	Refresh
	Selection Type	Region
	Region	Selected Segment

7.10 Add Button and a Process to Allow/Revoke Segment Access Right

This button will appear in the Selected Segment report region. When clicked, it will invoke the associated process to either allow or revoke access privilege to or from the selected group. Use Table 7-10 to create the button and the corresponding process.

Table 7-10. *Button and Process Attributes*

Action	Attribute	Value
Create Button	Name	Allow/Revoke
	Label	Allow/Revoke
	Region	Selected Segment
	Button Position	Next
	Hot	Yes
	Action	Submit Page
Add Page Process	Name	Update Allow_Access Column
	Type	PL/SQL Code
	PL/SQL Code	Book_Code\Chapter7\Allow Access.txt
	Point	Processing
	When Button Pressed	Allow/Revoke

7.11 Test Your Work

Execute the following steps to test your work:

1. Save your work, and execute the module from the Setup ➤ User Groups menu. The page resembling Figure 7-1 should come up.

2. Click the New option in the Parameters pane.

3. Enter a title for the new group. For example, enter **Admins**.

4. Click the button Create Group—Allow All. This should create the Admins group with all application privileges.

5. Click the Existing option, and select Admins from the select list. Click different tree nodes and watch the changes in the right pane.

    Click the Allow/Revoke button and note the immediate reflection.

    The value *Y* in the Allow Access column says that the selected group has the access privilege on the selected segment.

6. Add two more groups. Name the first one **Managers** and the second one **Clerks**. Create the Managers group using the Create Group—Allow All button. Create the Clerks group using the Create Group—Disallow All button.

Note   Sometimes when you click a segment node you do not see anything in the Selected Segment region; this happens when you forget to select a group from the select list.

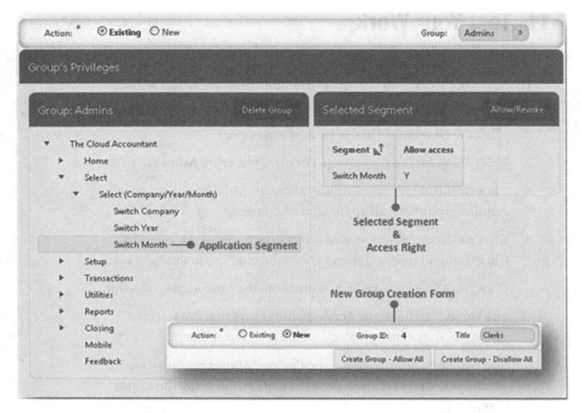

Figure 7-1. *Group's Privileges page*

7.12 Summary

You've successfully set up the application access privileges, but these privileges are not yet implemented. This is because the application is in the development phase and only after its completion will you be in a position to completely deploy the security module, which will be done in Chapter 31. In the next chapter, you will create a setup to add accounts of the application users.

CHAPTER 8

Create Users

After creating groups, you add users to them, as shown in Figure 8-1 later in this chapter. You input a user ID for each new user, but when you call up an existing user's record for modification, this value is displayed as read-only text. You also allocate a default company to each new user to work in. This allocation is helpful in restricting a user to handling the accounts of a specific company. You might notice from Figure 8-1 that besides assigning the Admins group, you also specify whether the user is an administrator. This is because you have a column (Admin) in the GL_USERS table that explicitly assigns administrative rights to those users marked as administrators, irrespective of the group to which they belong. This explicit marking is necessary in some cases to quickly assess whether a user is an administrator. You'll see an instance of this in the Chapter 9.

CREATE USERS

```
CREATE TABLE gl_users
(userID VARCHAR2(50), cocode NUMBER CONSTRAINT fk_users REFERENCES gl_
company (Cocode), coyear NUMBER(4), comonthid NUMBER(2), groupID NUMBER(4)
CONSTRAINT fk_users2 REFERENCES gl_groups_master(groupID),
password VARCHAR2(4000), admin VARCHAR2(1), CONSTRAINT gl_users_pk PRIMARY
KEY (userID) ENABLE)
```

Besides their usual credentials, this table will store company, year, and month information for each user. This information will be displayed through the Global Page on every application page so that users will know where their transactions are going to be saved. For more details, see Chapter 10.

© Riaz Ahmed 2019
R. Ahmed, *Cloud Computing Using Oracle Application Express*,
https://doi.org/10.1007/978-1-4842-4243-8_8

8.1 Create Pages

Select the Form option followed by Report with Form on Table to create Report and Form pages, as mentioned in Table 8-1.

Table 8-1. *Report and Form Page Attributes*

Page Type	Attribute	Value
Report Page	Page Number	22
	Page Name	Users Report
	Table/View Name	GL_USERS
	Navigation Preference	Identify an existing navigation menu entry for this page.
	Existing Navigation Menu Entry	Setup
	Report Columns	Select all columns
Form Page	Page Number	23
	Page Name	User Form
	Page Mode	Modal Dialog
	Primary Key Type	Managed by Database (ROWID)
	Form Columns	Select three columns: USERID, GROUPID, and ADMIN

After creation, modify both these pages to set the attributes listed in Table 8-2. The default query in the source SQL query is replaced with a custom join query, which fetches users' records from multiple tables.

Table 8-2. *Modified Page Attributes*

Action	Attribute	Value
Modify Region on Users Report Page (Report 1)	Title	Application Users
	SQL Query	Book_Code\Chapter8\SQL Query.txt
Modify Region on User Form Page	Region	Form on GL_USERS
	Title	Application User: &P23_USERID.

8.2 Create/Modify Items

Add and amend the items on page 23 using Table 8-3. The first item (Display Only) is added (between two existing items: User ID and Group ID) to show the ID of the selected user as read-only text. The condition for this item is set so that it will display only when you call a record of an existing user for modification. The opposite condition is set for the item P23_USERID to make it visible only for new records.

Table 8-3. *Create/Modify Items*

Action	Attribute	Value
Create Page Item	Item Name	P23_USERID2
	Type	Display Only
	Label	User ID:
	Sequence	25 (*between UserID and GroupID*)
	Template	Optional
	Source Type	Database Column
	Database Column	USERID
	Server-side Condition	Item Is NOT NULL
	Item	P23_USERID
Modify Item	Item Name	P23_USERID
	Type	Text Field
	Label	User ID:
	Template	Required
	Value Placeholder	Enter in UPPER CASE
	Server-side Condition	Item is NULL
	Item	P23_USERID
Modify Item	Item Name	P23_GROUPID
	Type	Select List
	Label	Group:

(continued)

Table 8-3. (*continued*)

Action	Attribute	Value
	Template	Required
	Value Required	Yes
	LOV Type	SQL Query
	SQL Query	SELECT groupTitle d, groupID r FROM gl_groups_master
Modify Item	Item Name	P23_ADMIN
	Type	Radio Group
	Label	Administrator:
	No. of Columns	2
	Template	Required
	LOV Type	Static Values
	Static Values	STATIC:Yes;Y,No;N
	Display Null Value	No
	Default Type	Static Value
	Static Value	N
Create Page Item	Item Name	P23_COMPANY
	Type	Select List
	Label	Default Company:
	Region	Application User: &P23_USERID.
	Template	Required
	Value Required	Yes
	LOV Type	Shared Component
	List of Values	COMPANIES
	Source Type	Database Column
	Database Column	COCODE

8.3 Create a Process to Set Company, Year, and Month

The process mentioned in Table 8-4 will be executed when either the CREATE or the APPLY CHANGES buttons are clicked on page 23. The process is added to fill in values for the company, year, and month columns based on the default company that is selected for a user. Create this process under the Processes node and place it just after the first process named Process Row of GL_USERS. If you place it in the last position, it won't execute because of the preceding Close Dialog process, which will execute before this process and will close the page.

Table 8-4. *Process Attributes*

Action	Attribute	Value
Create Process	Name	Set Company Year Month
	Type	PL/SQL Code
	PL/SQL Code	Book_Code\Chapter8\Company Year Month.txt
	Sequence	40 (Just after Process Row of GL_USERS process)
	Server-side Condition	Request is contained in Value
	Value	CREATE,SAVE (*case sensitive, must match button names*)

8.4 Test Your Work

Save your work and run the module from the Setup ➤ Users menu. You can view the two pages of the module in Figure 8-1.

1. Click the Create button.

2. Enter **SUPER** in UserID, set Group to Admins, select Yes for Administrator, set Default Company to ABC & Company, and click Create. Note that the password column of the new user will be blank at this stage. Setting user passwords is discussed in Chapter 9. Modify this user and take a look at the user ID, which should be displayed as an unmodifiable text.

3. Create two more users (belonging to different groups), as shown in Figure 8-1.

Figure 8-1. *Two pages of the module*

8.5 Summary

The users you created in this chapter are the holy souls who can access your application. In Chapter 9, you will create a form to set/reset their passwords.

CHAPTER 9

Reset Password

A user who wants to access this application can do so only with a valid ID and password. You created some user accounts in the previous chapter and assigned them IDs and groups. In this chapter, you will create a facility for setting and changing passwords. Note that this feature will be invoked from the Utilities menu. The Reset Password interface is self-explanatory. Administrators select a user ID and then provide and confirm a new password for it. The application then checks to make sure both of these are identical and, if so, allocates the password to the user ID. Users may also use the same method to reset an existing password. The initial password allocation task is performed by the application administrator.

9.1 Add Custom Functions

The users you created in the previous chapter reside in the database table GL_USERS without passwords; therefore, none of them can access the application at the moment. You'll create the password interface by adding a blank page to the application, but first you have to add two custom functions, CUSTOM_AUTH and CUSTOM_HASH, to your database. After receiving login information, the APEX engine evaluates and executes the authentication scheme that will be configured at the end of this chapter. The scheme makes a call to a function named CUSTOM_AUTH, which, in conjunction with the CUSTOM_HASH function, authenticates users using the credentials stored in the GL_USERS table. The two functions are added to the database to implement a custom authentication mechanism. The CUSTOM_HASH function is a subordinate function to the CUSTOM_AUTH

© Riaz Ahmed 2019
R. Ahmed, *Cloud Computing Using Oracle Application Express*,
https://doi.org/10.1007/978-1-4842-4243-8_9

function and is called from the parent function to obfuscate passwords with hash algorithm. Execute the following steps to add these two functions to the database:

1. Open the SQL Commands interface from SQL Workshop.

2. Copy and paste the two functions available in the `Chapter9\ Custom Functions.txt` file and click the Run button to store them in the database. If you are using the online APEX version, then create the functions provided in the CustomFunctions.txt file, which uses the `DBMS_OBFUSCATION_TOOLKIT` package. For an offline APEX version, use the `Custom_Functions_DBMS_CRYPTO. txt` file.

3. For verification, open the Object Browser interface and locate the two functions in the Functions category, as shown Figure 9-1.

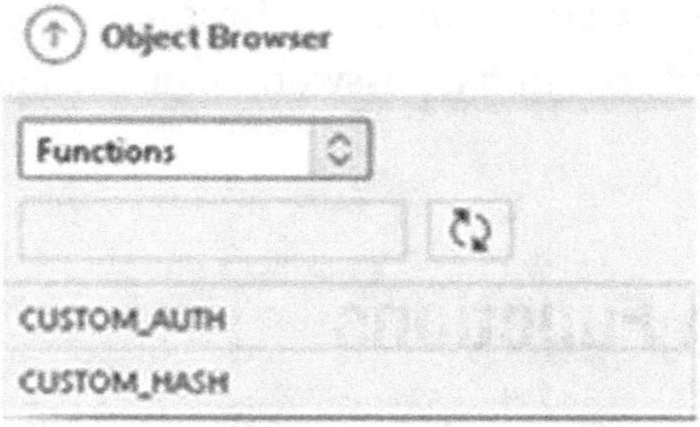

Figure 9-1. *Functions category*

Note that the `DBMS_OBFUSCATION_TOOLKIT` package has been deprecated in favor of `DBMS_CRYPTO`, which is now used to encrypt and decrypt data. It provides support for various industry-standard encryption and hashing algorithms, including the highly secure Advanced Encryption Standard (AES) encryption algorithm. AES has been approved as a new standard to replace the Data Encryption Standard (DES).

Oracle Database installs the `DBMS_CRYPTO` package in the SYS schema. In order to use this package, users must be granted access to it, as shown here:

```
conn sys/******** as sysdba
grant execute on sys.dbms_crypto to <user>;
```

Note that you do not have access to the SYS schema in the online APEX version, so you can't use DMBS_CRYPTO.

In a production environment, where you have access to the SYS schema, run the two functions provided in the Custom_Functions_DBMS_CRYPTO.txt file in the user's schema to use DMBS_CRYPTO instead of the DBMS_OBFUSCATION_TOOLKIT package.

9.2 Create Page

Create the password interface using a blank page and then set the attributes listed in Table 9-1. Note that this page will be called from the Reset Password option in the Utilities menu. The query defined in the SQL Query attribute for the Select List (P56_USERID) uses a condition in the WHERE clause (admin='Y') to quickly assess the presence of an administrator, who is allowed to change the password of any user. This is the reason for the inclusion of the Admin column in the GL_USERS table. By setting this condition, the Select List item, which is added to display a list of all users, will be visible to administrators only. Normal users will see only their own user ID in the display item named P56_USERID2.

Table 9-1. *Page Attributes*

Action	Attribute	Value
Create Page	Page Number	56
	Name	Reset Password
	Page Mode	Normal
	Breadcrumb	—Don't use breadcrumbs on page—
	Navigation Preference	Identify an existing navigation menu entry for this page.
	Existing Navigation Menu Entry	Utilities
Create Region	Title	Reset Password
	Type	Static Content
	Template	Standard

(continued)

Table 9-1. (*continued*)

Action	Attribute	Value
Create Page Item	Name	P56_USERID
	Type	Select List
	Label	User ID:
	Region	Reset Password
	LOV Type	SQL Query
	SQL Query	SELECT userid d, userid r FROM gl_users
	Server-side Condition	Rows Returned
	SQL Query	SELECT 1 FROM gl_users WHERE userid = :APP_USER AND admin = 'Y'

In Table 9-2, the Display Only item (P56_USERID2) will show the ID of the current nonadmin user using a substitution string (&APP_USER.). The Save Session State attribute is set to YES to store the current item value in the session state when the page gets submitted. If set to No, you'll encounter the error message "No user selected for the reset password process." You also used an opposite WHERE clause in the condition query, in contrast to the previous one, to display nonadmin IDs. Finally, you added two password page items. The first one is used to enter the new password, whereas the other one is added for its confirmation.

Table 9-2. *Items and Button Attributes*

Action	Attribute	Value
Create Page Item	Name	P56_USERID2
	Type	Display Only
	Label	User ID:
	Save Session State	Yes
	Region	Reset Password
	Default Type	Static Value

(*continued*)

Table 9-2. (*continued*)

Action	Attribute	Value
	Static Value	&APP_USER.
	Server-side Condition	Rows Returned
	SQL Query	SELECT 1 FROM gl_users WHERE userid = :APP_USER AND admin != 'Y'
Create Page Item	Name	P56_PASSWORD1
	Type	Password
	Label	New Password:
	Submit When Enter Pressed	No
	Region	Reset Password
	Template	Required
	Value Required	Yes
Create Page Item	Name	P56_PASSWORD2
	Type	Password
	Label	Confirm Password:
	Submit When Enter Pressed	No
	Region	Reset Password
	Template	Required
	Value Required	Yes
Create Button	Name	RESET_PW
	Label	Reset Password
	Region	Reset Password
	Button Position	Copy
	Hot	Yes
	Action	Submit Page

Note   Upon page submission, the RESET_PW button will run the Update Password process.

9.3 Check User ID and Match Password Validations

In Table 9-3, the first validation checks for the existence of a user ID, while the second one checks for a match.

Table 9-3. *Validation Attributes*

Action	Attribute	Value
Create Validation	Name	Check User ID
	Type	PL/SQL Function (returning Error Text)
	PL/SQL Function	Book_Code\Chapter9\Check User ID.txt
	When Button Pressed	RESET_PW
Create Validation	Name	Match Passwords
	Type	PL/SQL Function Body (returning Boolean)
	PL/SQL Function	Book_Code\Chapter9\Match Passwords.txt
	Error Message	Passwords do not match
	When Button Pressed	RESET_PW

9.4 Update Password Process

The process specified in Table 9-4 will store a new password for the selected user.

Table 9-4. *Update Password Process Attributes*

Action	Attribute	Value
Create Process	Name	Update Password
	Type	PL/SQL Code
	PL/SQL Code	Book_Code\Chapter9\Update Password.txt
	Point	Processing
	Success Message	Password changed successfully
	Error Message	Could not change password
	When Button Pressed	RESET_PW

If you run the page at this stage, you won't see the user's select list. This is because the select list item, P56_USERID, is visible only when the currently logged in user is an administrator. Since the account you are currently logged in with doesn't exist in the GL_USERS table, the list doesn't appear. To make the list visible, create an admin account for yourself having the same ID you are currently using from the Users option in the Setup menu. After creating your new account, invoke the Reset Password page to test your work by setting passwords for all application users, including yourself. Note that the passwords you set through this interface are case-sensitive; therefore, care must be taken of when saving them. Verify the addition of passwords to the table by accessing the table either from the Object Browser utility in SQL Workshop or through the user report page from the Users menu.

9.5 Change Authentication Scheme

At this stage you can set and browse the users' passwords, but you cannot use these passwords to log in. This is because of the currently implemented authentication scheme, which was set to the Application Express Scheme when you initially created the application. To authenticate the users through their new IDs and passwords, you have to create a custom authentication scheme. Here are the steps to implement this scheme:

1. Select Authentication Scheme from Shared Components.

2. Click the Create button.

3. Select the option Based on the preconfigured scheme from the gallery and click Next.

4. Enter Custom Scheme in the Name box and select Custom as the Scheme Type. On the same page, enter **CUSTOM_AUTH** for the Authentication Function Name attribute. This is the name of the function that you created earlier in this chapter to verify users' credentials on the login page.

5. Click the Create Authentication Scheme button. The new scheme will appear on the page with a check mark. Now you can access the application using the credentials stored in the GL_USERS table. Access the Reset Password page, which should look like Figure 9-2.

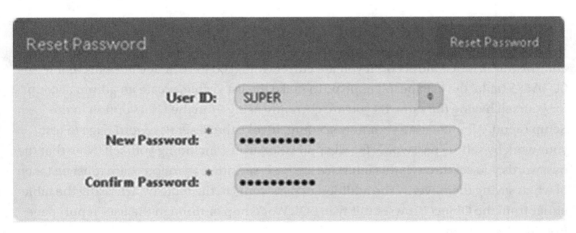

Figure 9-2. *Reset Password page*

9.6 Summary

Now that you have allowed your users to access the application, you must also allow privileged users to switch company, year, and month, which comes next.

CHAPTER 10

Switch Company, Year, and Month

This page allows users to switch the company, year, and month depending on their access privileges. Recall that every new user was allotted a default company, while an associated process saved a default year and month within their profiles so that they could start using the application right away. These selections are saved in the GL_USERS table and are reflected on the top-right corner of every page through the Global Page.

10.1 Create Page

This segment will be created using a blank page. After creating the blank page, add page components, as listed in Table 10-1. The last two select lists added to the page use an attribute called Cascading LOV Parent Item(s). This attribute is used to associate an LOV to its parent. For example, when you select a company, the second list is refreshed to display years of the selected company. Similarly, the third list gets populated with the corresponding months of the selected company.

© Riaz Ahmed 2019
R. Ahmed, *Cloud Computing Using Oracle Application Express,*
https://doi.org/10.1007/978-1-4842-4243-8_10

Table 10-1. *Page Attributes*

Action	Attribute	Value
Create Page	Page Number	30
	Name	Select
	Page Mode	Normal
	Breadcrumb	—Don't use breadcrumbs on page—
	Navigation Preference	Identify an existing navigation menu entry for this page
	Existing Navigation Menu Entry	Select
Create Region	Title	Select
	Type	Static Content
	Template	Standard
Create Page Item	Name	P30_COMPANY
	Type	Select List
	Label	Company
	Region	Select
	Template	Required
	Value Required	Yes
	LOV Type	SQL Query
	SQL Query	SELECT coname, cocode FROM gl_company ORDER BY cocode
	Source Type	SQL Query (return single value)
	SQL Query	SELECT cocode FROM gl_users WHERE userid = :APP_USER
	Source Used	Always, replacing any existing value in session state

(continued)

Table 10-1. (*continued*)

Action	Attribute	Value
Create Page Item	Name	P30_YEAR
	Type	Select List
	Label	\Year\
	Region	Select
	Template	Required
	Value Required	Yes
	LOV Type	SQL Query
	SQL Query	SELECT DISTINCT(coyear) d, coyear r FROM gl_fiscal_year WHERE cocode=:P30_COMPANY ORDER BY coyear
	Cascading LOV Parent Item(s)	P30_COMPANY
	Source Type	SQL Query (return single value)
	SQL Query	SELECT coyear FROM gl_users WHERE userid = :APP_USER
	Source Used	Always, replacing any existing value in session state

(*continued*)

Table 10-1. (*continued*)

Action	Attribute	Value
Create Page Item	Name	P30_MONTH
	Type	Select List
	Label	Month
	Region	Select
	Template	Required
	Value Required	Yes
	LOV Type	SQL Query
	SQL Query	SELECT DISTINCT(comonthname) d, comonthid r FROM gl_fiscal_year WHERE cocode=:P30_COMPANY ORDER BY comonthid
	Cascading LOV Parent Item(s)	P30_COMPANY
	Source Type	SQL Query (return single value)
	SQL Query	SELECT comonthid FROM gl_users WHERE userid = :APP_USER
	Source Used	Always, replacing any existing value in session state

10.2 Add Button

The button in Table 10-2 will submit the page to update the user's profile, using the process mentioned in Table 10-4.

Table 10-2. *Button Attributes*

Action	Attribute	Value
Create Button	Button Name	Select
	Label	Select
	Region	Select
	Button Position	Copy
	Hot	Yes
	Action	Submit Page

10.3 Add Validations

The three validations in Table 10-3 are included to check the switching privileges of a user for the three options.

Table 10-3. *Validation Attributes*

Action	Attribute	Value
Create Validation	Name	Check Switch Company Privilege
	Type	PL/SQL Function (returning Error Text)
	PL/SQL Function	Book_Code\Chapter10\Switch Company.txt
	When Button Pressed	Select *(not-select-)*
Create Validation	Name	Check Switch Year Privilege
	Type	PL/SQL Function (returning Error Text)
	PL/SQL Function	Book_Code\Chapter10\Switch Year.txt
	When Button Pressed	Select *(not-select-)*
Create Validation	Name	Check Switch Month Privilege
	Type	PL/SQL Function (returning Error Text)
	PL/SQL Function	Book_Code\Chapter10\Switch Month. txt
	When Button Pressed	Select *(not-select-)*

10.4 Update User Profile Process

After passing the previous validations, the process specified in Table 10-4 is executed to store new values in the GL_USERS table.

Table 10-4. *Update User Profile Process*

Action	Attribute	Value
Create Process	Name	Update User Profile
	Type	PL/SQL Code
	PL/SQL Code	UPDATE gl_users SET cocode=:P30_COMPANY, coyear=:P30_YEAR, comonthid=:P30_MONTH WHERE upper(userid)=upper(:APP_USER);
	Point	Processing
	Success Message	Company/Year/Month switched successfully.
	Error Message	Could not switch company/year/month.
	When Button Pressed	Select

10.5 Display Company, Year, and Month

The page is ready for a test run. Although you can change all three options as a privileged user, there is no way to know whether the changes have taken place, except for looking at the GL_USERS table. In this section, you will make these selections visible on every application page so that users can see the company, year, and month they are working in. You will make use of a Global Page for this purpose. Open the Global Page (Page 0), which is created by default when you created a new application. Add components listed in Table 10-5 to the Global Page.

Table 10-5. *Global Page Attributes*

Action	Attribute	Value
Create Region	Title	User Profile
	Type	Static Content
	Position	Breadcrumb Bar
	Template	Blank with Attributes
	Server-side Condition	Current Page != Page (*the region will not appear on the login page*)
	Page	9999 (ID of the login page)
Create Page Item	Name	P0_USERPROFILE
	Type	Display Only
	Label	*Clear Label*
	Region	User Profile
	Custom Attributes	style="background:red; fontweight:bold; fontsize: 20; color:white;"
	Source Type	PL/SQL Function Body
	PL/SQL Function Body	Book_Code\Chapter10\User Profile.txt
	Source Used	Always, replacing any existing value in session state

Everything is set! Run this page (illustrated in Figure 10-1) from the Select menu, change the three options, and see the impact in the user profile region, which should now be visible on every application page.

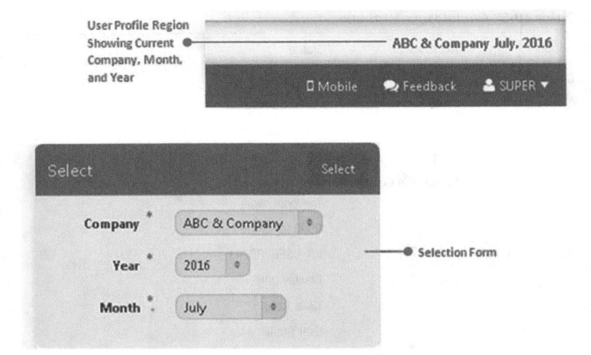

Figure 10-1. *Page to switch company, year, and month*

Note   The Year value shown in the user profile region displays the first part of the fiscal year, which is fetched from the financial year table. For example, the value shown in Figure 10-1 (top) represents 2015–2016. A fiscal year starting from July 1, 2015, and ending on June 30, 2016, will be displayed as 2015 for all 12 months, even for January 2016 and onward.

10.6 Summary

Users can access the application and can select their respective companies and fiscal years to post transactions. By creating the cost center setup in the next chapter, you allow these users to lay the foundation of the data entry process.

CHAPTER 11

Cost Centers

Cost and revenue centers help you maintain accounts of all departments and divisions participating in your business. Using this setup, you keep track of revenues generated by departments and expenses incurred by them. After creating cost centers, you can link them to the main financial accounts in the chart of accounts. This allows you to set a default cost/revenue center for every financial account. When you pick up an account from the chart of accounts during the voucher generation process, these cost/revenue centers come along as default entries to minimize data entry work.

COST CENTERS TABLE

```
CREATE TABLE GL_Cost_Center
(Cocode NUMBER CONSTRAINT fk_cost_center REFERENCES GL_Company (Cocode),
Cccode VARCHAR2(5),
Cctitle VARCHAR2(25), Cclevel NUMBER(1),
CONSTRAINT GL_COST_CENTER_PK PRIMARY KEY (Cocode,Cccode) ENABLE)
```

11.1 Create Pages

Create a Form page followed by the Report with Form on Table option. Using Table 11-1, set the attributes for the two pages.

© Riaz Ahmed 2019
R. Ahmed, *Cloud Computing Using Oracle Application Express*,
https://doi.org/10.1007/978-1-4842-4243-8_11

Table 11-1. *Two Page Attributes*

Page Type	Attribute	Value
Report Page	Page Number	13
	Page Name	Cost Centers Report
	Table/View Name	GL_COST_CENTER
	Navigation Preference	Identify an existing navigation menu entry for this page.
	Existing Navigation Menu Entry	Setup
	Report Columns	Select 3 columns: CCCODE,CCTITLE, and CCLEVEL
Form Page	Page Number	14
	Page Name	Cost Centers Form
	Page Mode	Modal Dialog
	Primary Key Type	Managed by Database (ROWID)
	Form Columns	Select 3 columns: CCCODE,CCTITLE, and CCLEVEL

After creation, modify the report page (13) to alter the default SQL statement. A WHERE clause is added to the default SQL query (indicated in Table 11-2), which fetches the current company's cost centers.

Table 11-2. *Modified Query*

Action	Attribute	Value
Modify Region	Region	Cost Centers Setup
	SQL Query	SELECT "ROWID", "CCCODE","CCTITLE","CCLEVEL" FROM "#OWNER#"."GL_COST_CENTER" **WHERE cocode = (select cocode from gl_users where userid = :app_user)**

11.2 Delete Processes

Remove the two default processes (Process Row of GL_COST_CENTER and reset page) from page 14, along with the CREATE and APPLY CHANGES buttons. You'll create custom processes and add a new button to handle these operations.

11.3 Modify Delete Button

On page 14, modify the Delete button (which was created by the wizard) using the attributes mentioned in Table 11-3. You use a JavaScript function to present a confirmation box before deleting a record. Note that the visibility of this button and the corresponding delete process is controlled by a condition set on this page, which states that this button will be visible only when the P14_ROWID page item is NOT NULL—in other words, when the record is fetched from page 13 for modification. You also disable the default database action (SQL DELETE action) because you handle this process manually; see Table 11-13.

Table 11-3. *Modified Delete Button*

Action	Attribute	Value
Modify Button	Button Name	DELETE
	Action	Redirect to URL
	Target	javascript:apex.confirm('Are you sure you wish delete this record?','DELETE');
	Execute Validations	Yes
	Database Action	-Select-

11.4 Add Button

Add a new button to page 14 using Table 11-4 to handle new and amended records.

Table 11-4. *New Button Attributes*

Action	Attribute	Value	Attribute	Value
Create Button	Name	Save	Button Position	Create
	Label	Save	Hot	Yes
	Region	Buttons	Action	Submit Page

11.5 Modify Page Items

Modify page 14 items using Table 11-5. Note that the Level column will be displayed as a read-only item.

Table 11-5. *Modified Page Item Attributes*

Action	Attribute	Value
Modify Item	Name	P14_CCCODE
	Type	Text Field
	Label	Code
	Template	Required
	Value Required	Yes
	Width/Maximum Length	5
Modify Item	Name	P14_CCTITLE
	Template	Required
	Value Required	Yes
Modify Item	Name	P14_CCLEVEL
	Type	Display Only
	Template	Required
	Save Session State	No

11.6 Add Dynamic Action: Evaluate Level

The dynamic action specified in Table 11-6 will be created on page 14 to calculate a level for each cost center account. Note that this setup comprises two levels. The first level, which denotes locations, is two digits long (99), while the second one, which represents departments or divisions, carries five digits (99999). The first two digits in the second level represent its parent level.

Table 11-6. *Dynamic Action Attributes*

Action	Attribute	Value	Attribute	Value
Create Dynamic Action	Name	Evaluate Level	PL/SQL Code	Book_Code\Chapter11\
	Event	Lose Focus		Evaluate Level.txt
	Selection Type	Item(s)	Page Items to Submit	P14_CCCODE
	Item(s)	P14_CCTITLE	Page Items to Return	P14_CCLEVEL
	Action (under Show)	Execute PL/SQL Code	Fire on Initialization	Yes

11.7 Validation: Check Level

The validation specified in Table 11-7 will check whether the value of the account level is zero. Note that the valid values for this item are 1 and 2 only. The dynamic action created in the previous section will calculate this value automatically.

Table 11-7. *Validation: Check Level*

Action	Attribute	Value
Create Validation	Name	Check Level
	Validation Type	Item is NOT zero
	Item	P14_CCLEVEL
	Error Message	You've defined an invalid Cost Center code.
	When Button Pressed	Save

11.8 Validation: Check Parent Level

As the name suggests, the validation specified in Table 11-8 is added to check the parent level of an account. To implement application integrity, you are not allowed to create an account without a parent. For example, in the current setup, a department cannot be created without first creating a location.

Table 11-8. *Validation: Check Parent Level*

Action	Attribute	Value
Create Validation	Name	Check Parent Level
	Type	PL/SQL Function Body (returning Boolean)
	PL/SQL Function	Book_Code\Chapter11\ Check Parent Level.txt
	Error Message	Parent level not found.
	When Button Pressed	Save

Note   Duplicate cost center code is eliminated by the table constraint (GL_COST_ CENTER_PK PRIMARY KEY (Cocode,Cccode)), which shows the generic message "An error occurred while saving Cost Center record when you try to enter a code which already exists." To inform the user about the actual problem, you can create a validation to search the table for an existing cost center code prior to saving a record.

11.9 Validation: Check Child Level

Just like you checked for the existence of the parent level while *creating a new* child account, the validation in Table 11-9 will check for the existence of a child account before *deleting* a parent level account.

Table 11-9. *Validation: Check Child Level*

Action	Attribute	Value
Create Validation	Name	Check Child Level
	Type	PL/SQL Function Body (returning Boolean)
	PL/SQL Function	Book_Code\Chapter11\Check Child Level.txt
	Error Message	Child account found. Unable to delete cost center record.
	When Button Pressed	DELETE

11.10 Validation: Check in Transaction

An account used even in a single transaction must not be deleted. The validation in Table 11-10 is added for this purpose. Note that in this application you will use the last level (in other words, level 2) in your transactions to allocate cost centers.

Table 11-10. *Validation: Check in Transaction*

Action	Attribute	Value
Create Validation	Name	Check in Transaction
	Type	PL/SQL Function Body (returning Boolean)
	PL/SQL Function	Book_Code\Chapter11\Check in Transaction.txt
	Error Message	Account used in transaction. Unable to delete cost center record.
	When Button Pressed	DELETE

11.11 Validation: Disallow Code Modification

Cost centers are rendered in a text item that an end user can easily modify. The validation specified in Table 11-11 will prevent the code from being modified in order to retain application consistency. The condition set for this validation checks for a value in the hidden item (P14_ROWID). A non-null value in this item indicates that a record exists on the page with its code.

Table 11-11. *Validation: Disallow Code Modification*

Action	Attribute	Value
Create Validation	Name	Disallow Code Modification
	Type	PL/SQL Function Body (returning Boolean)
	PL/SQL Function	Book_Code\Chapter11\Disallow Code Modification.txt
	Error Message	Cost Center code cannot be modified.
	When Button Pressed	Save
	Server-side Condition	Item is NOT NULL
	Item	P14_ROWID

11.12 Process: Save Record

The process being created in Table 11-12 is the one that will save a cost center record. Note that this process will handle both new and updated cost centers.

Table 11-12. *Process: Save Record Attributes*

Action	Attribute	Value
Create Process	Name	Save Record
	Type	PL/SQL Code
	PL/SQL Code	Book_Code\Chapter11\Save Record.txt
	Sequence	10
	Point	Processing
	Success Message	Cost Center record saved.
	Error Message	An error occurred while saving Cost Center record.
	When Button Pressed	Save

11.13 Process: Delete Record

This process mentioned in Table 11-13 will delete a cost center record after passing all validations.

Table 11-13. *Delete Record Process Attributes*

Action	Attribute	Value
Create Process	Name	Delete Record
	Type	PL/SQL Code
	PL/SQL Code	DELETE FROM gl_cost_center WHERE CCcode=:P14_CCcode AND cocode=(SELECT cocode FROM gl_users WHERE userid = :app_user);
	Sequence	20 (*to execute before the Close Dialog process*)
	Point	Processing
	Success Message	Cost Center record deleted.
	Error Message	An error occurred while deleting Cost Center record.
	When Button Pressed	DELETE

Remove the CREATE Process Attributes and SAVE button values from the request specified in the Close Dialog process to generate continuous cost center records. In the Processing tab, click the Close Dialog process. Scroll down to the Condition section in the properties editor, and remove the CREATE and SAVE entries from the Value list. By default, the modal page is closed when the Create, Save, or Delete buttons are clicked. By removing the CREATE and SAVE entries, the dialog page will be closed only when the Delete button is clicked.

11.14 Add Button: Refresh

Create a button on page 13 using the attributes listed in Table 11-14 to refresh the Cost Centers report.

Table 11-14. *Refresh Button Attributes*

Attribute	Value
Button Name	Refresh
Label	Refresh
Region	Report 1
Button Position	Top of Region
Button Template	Text with Icon
Hot	No
Icon	fa-undo
Action	Submit Page

11.15 Test Your Work

After saving your work, execute the following steps to create cost centers in the application:

1. Run the module from the Setup | Cost Centers menu. Figure 11-1 illustrates the two pages of this module.

2. Click Create on page 13.

3. Enter **01** in Code and **Head Office** in Title.

4. Click the Save button. This will add a new cost center level one record.

5. Create a new record by entering **01001** for Code and **Admin** for Title. Click Save. This will create the Admin department under the Head Office location. Note that the levels for both these accounts are assessed automatically by the dynamic action created through Table 11-6.

6. Using the file Cost Centers.xls, in the Book_Code\Chapter11 folder, create the remaining cost centers. The last entry ("09-N/A - not applicable") in the XLS file will be used for all financial accounts in the Chart of Accounts (coming up next) where cost centers are inapplicable.

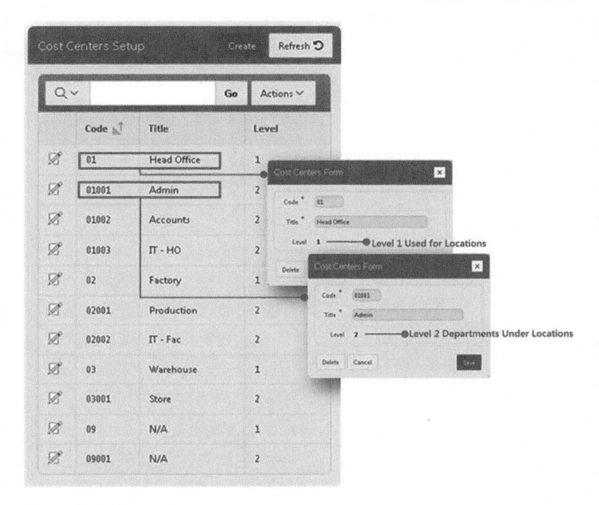

Figure 11-1. *Cost centers pages*

11.16 Summary

The cost center is a handy setup for organizations that want to keep track of income and expenses. In the next chapter, you will create the heart of financial accounting called the *chart of accounts*.

CHAPTER 12

Chart of Accounts

The chart of accounts (COA) is part of the application that needs to be planned carefully before implementation. A well-planned COA provides better insight into the financial matters of an organization. A separate COA is created for each company; however, you can create a COA for one company—the master COA—and then copy it to the others using the Copy COA utility as developed in the next chapter. The accounts created here are selected for each transaction during voucher generation, report calls, and preparation of financial statements. Because this setup is similar to the cost center setup, you will use the copy utility to save some time. The account code used in this setup uses the format 9-99-999-99999, which contains four separate number groupings or levels. The first level defines the nature of account, while the next three levels act as its subcategories. Each account specified on the first level belongs to one of the following natures: equities, liabilities, assets, revenues, and expenses. The initial three levels are called *group levels*, whereas the bottom level (in other words, level 4) is called the *transaction level* because accounts from this level are selected to generate transactions in the vouchers interface. The group-level accounts are used in trial balance and financial statement reports to extract summarized group-level information.

Here is the COA table:

```
CREATE TABLE GL_COA
(Cocode NUMBER CONSTRAINT fk_coa REFERENCES GL_Company (Cocode), COAcode
VARCHAR2(11),
COAtitle VARCHAR2(50), COAlevel NUMBER(1), COAnature VARCHAR2(11), COAtype
VARCHAR2(11), Cccode VARCHAR2(5), CONSTRAINT GL_COA_PK PRIMARY KEY
(Cocode,COAcode) ENABLE)
```

© Riaz Ahmed 2019
R. Ahmed, *Cloud Computing Using Oracle Application Express*,
https://doi.org/10.1007/978-1-4842-4243-8_12

12.1 Create Three Lists of Values

Create three LOVs from scratch using Tables 12-1 to 12-3. The first one will show departments (level 2) from the cost centers table for association with financial accounts. This association is not mandatory. The second LOV contains the five natures mentioned earlier for assignment to the first level. The third LOV is created to identify bank accounts. It will be visible for the last level only. All accounts marked as "Bank" type in the COA will be used in Chapter 21. Accounts other than banks will be marked as "Others," for distinction. Take a look at the COA.xls file provided in the downloaded code's Chapter 12 folder. Table 12-1 shows attributes for the Cost Center LOV.

Table 12-1. *Cost Center LOV*

Attribute	Value
Name	Cost Centers
Type	Dynamic
Query	`SELECT cccode||'-'||cctitle t, cccode c FROM gl_cost_center WHERE cclevel=2 AND cocode=(select cocode from gl_userswhere userid=:APP_USER) ORDER BY 1`

1. Set the Name of the second LOV to COA Nature and its Type to Static.

Table 12-2. *COA Nature LOV*

Display Value	Return Value
Capital	Capital
Liabilities	Liabilities
Assets	Assets
Revenues	Revenues
Expenses	Expenses

2.   Set the Name of the third LOV to COA Types and its Type to Static.

Table 12-3. *COA Type LOV*

Display Value	Return Value
Bank	Bank
Others	Others

12.2 Create Pages

Create a Form page followed by the Report with Form on Table option. Using Table 12-4, set the attributes for the two pages.

Table 12-4. *Two Page Attributes*

Page Type	Attribute	Value
Report Page	Report Page Number	15
	Report Page Name	COA Report
	Table/View Name	GL_COA
	Navigation Preference	Identify an existing navigation menu entry for this page.
	Existing Navigation Menu Entry	Setup
	Report Columns	Select all columns
Form Page	Form Page Number	16
	Form Page Name	COA Form
	Form Page Mode	Modal Dialog
	Primary Key Type	Managed by Database (ROWID)
	Form Columns	Select all columns

12.3 Modify the Report Page (Page 15)

Modify the COA report page by setting the attributes listed in Table 12-5.

Table 12-5. *COA Report Page Modified*

Action	Attribute	Value
Modify Region	Region	Report 1
	Title	Chart of Accounts
	SQL Query	SELECT "ROWID", "COACODE", "COATITLE", "COALEVEL", "COANATURE", "COATYPE", "CCCODE" FROM "#OWNER#"."GL_COA" WHERE cocode = (select cocode from gl_users whereuserid = :app_user) ORDER BY coacode

12.4 Modify the Form Page (Page 16)

Modify the COA form page by setting the attributes listed in Table 12-6. Change the
Region Title attribute to COA Form.

Table 12-6. *Modify COA Form Page*

Action	Attribute	Value
Modify Page Item	Name	P16_COACODE
	Type	Text Field
	Label	Code
	Template	Required
	Width	11
	Value Required	Yes
	Maximum Length	11

(continued)

Table 12-6. (*continued*)

Action	Attribute	Value
Modify Page Item	Name	P16_COATITLE
	Label	Title
	Template	Required
	Width	50
	Value Required	Yes
	Maximum Length	50
Modify Page Item	Name	P16_COALEVEL
	Label	Level
	Type	Display Only
	Save Session State	No
	Template	Optional
Modify Page Item	Name	P16_COANATURE
	Type	Select List
	Label	Nature
	Template	Optional
	Value Required	No (*because nature is not required for levels greater than 1*)
	LOV Type	Shared Component
	Shared Component	COA NATURE
	Display Null Value	No
	Source Type	Database Column
	Database Column	COANATURE
	Source Used	Always, replacing any existing value in session state

(*continued*)

Table 12-6. (*continued*)

Action	Attribute	Value
Modify Page Item	Name	P16_COATYPE
	Type	Select List
	Label	Account Type
	Template	Optional
	Value Required	No (*because it is not required for levels 1 through 3*)
	LOV Type	Shared Component
	Shared Component	COA TYPES
	Display Extra Values	No
	Display Null Value	Yes
	Source Type	Database Column
	Database Column	COATYPE
	Source Used	Always, replacing any existing value in session state
Modify Page Item	Name	P16_CCCODE
	Type	Popup LOV
	Label	Cost Center
	Template	Optional
	Value Required	No
	LOV Type	Shared Component
	Shared Component	COST CENTERS
	Source Type	Database Column
	Database Column	CCCODE
	Source Used	Always, replacing any existing value in session state

(*continued*)

Table 12-6. (*continued*)

Action	Attribute	Value
Create Page Item	Name	P16_NATURE_DISPLAY
	Type	Display Only
	Label	Nature
	Save Session State	No
	Sequence	65 (to place it just under P16_COANATURE)
	Region	COA Form
	Template	Optional
	Source Type	Null

12.5 Create Dynamic Actions

Create the following dynamic actions for this module.

Table 12-7. *Evaluate Level Dynamic Action*

Action	Attribute	Value
Create Dynamic Action	Name	Evaluate Level
	Event	Lose Focus
	Selection Type	Item(s)
	Item(s)	P16_COACODE
	Action (under Show)	Execute PL/SQL Code
	PL/SQL Code	Book_Code\Chapter12\Evaluate Level.txt
	Page Items to Submit	P16_COACODE
	Page Items to Return	P16_COALEVEL
	Fire on Initialization	Yes

The dynamic actions will show/hide P16_COANATURE and other page items when the value of the Level page item changes.

Table 12-8. *Hide Show Dynamic Action*

Action	Attribute	Value
Create Dynamic Action	Name	Hide Show Item
	Event	Change
	Selection Type	Item(s)
	Item	P16_COALEVEL
Client-side Condition	Type	Item=Value
	Item	P16_COALEVEL
	Value	1

Note   The previous condition is set for the dynamic action. It says the following:

```
If P16_COALEVEL=1 then
  Show: P16_COANATURE and
  Hide: P16_NATURE_DISPLAY,P16_COATYPE,P16_CCCODE
Else
  Hide: P16_COANATURE
```

Table 12-9 shows the true action attributes.

Table 12-9. *True Action Attributes*

Attribute	Value
Action	Show
Selection Type	Item(s)
Item(s)	P16_COANATURE (*this is the page element to control*)
Fire on Initialization	Yes

Now, right-click the False node, and select Create False Action. Set the attributes in Table 12-10 for the False action.

Table 12-10. *False Action Attributes*

Attribute	Value
Action	Hide
Selection Type	Item(s)
Item(s)	P16_COANATURE
Fire on Initialization	Yes

Add another True action under the True node using the attributes in Table 12-11.

Table 12-11. *Second True Action Attributes*

Attribute	Value
Action	Hide
Selection Type	Item(s)
Item(s)	P16_NATURE_DISPLAY,P16_COATYPE,P16_CCCODE
Fire on Initialization	Yes

Create the dynamic action in Table 12-12 to show/hide the Type and Cost Center items when the value of level is 4.

Table 12-12. *Show Type and Cost Center Dynamic Action*

Attribute	Value
Name	Show Type and Cost Center
Event	Change
Selection Type	Item(s)
Item	P16_COALEVEL
Client-side Condition	
Type	Item=Value
Item	P16_COALEVEL
Value	4

Note   The condition says the following:

```
If P16_COALEVEL=4 then
  Show: P16_COATYPE,P16_CCCODE
Else
  Hide: P16_COATYPE,P16_CCCODE
```

Table 12-13 shows the true action attributes.

Table 12-13. *True Action Attributes*

Attribute	Value
Action	Show
Selection Type	Item(s)
Item(s)	P16_COATYPE, P16_CCCODE
Fire on Initialization	Yes

Right-click the False node, and select Create False Action. Set the attributes in Table 12-14 for the False action.

Table 12-14. *False Action Attributes*

Attribute	Value
Action	Hide
Selection Type	Item(s)
Item(s)	P16_COATYPE, P16_CCCODE
Fire on Initialization	Yes

Evaluate and turn the account nature into a display-only item based on the first level, for level numbers 2, 3, and 4, as shown in Table 12-15.

Table 12-15. *Evaluate Nature Item Dynamic Action*

Attribute	Value
Name	Evaluate Nature
Event	Lose Focus
Selection Type	Item(s)
Item(s)	P16_COACODE
Action (*under Show node*)	Execute PL/SQL Code
PL/SQL Code	Book_Code\Chapter12\Evaluate Nature.txt
Page Items to Submit	P16_COACODE
Page Items to Return	P16_NATURE_DISPLAY
Fire on Initialization	Yes

12.6 Create Validations

Create the following validations to store legitimate chart of accounts data in the database.

Table 12-16. *Validation: Check Level*

Attribute	Value
Name	Check Level
Validation Type	Item is NOT zero
Item	P16_COALEVEL
Error Message	You've defined an invalid account code.
When Button Pressed	SAVE

Table 12-17. *Validation: Check Parent Level*

Attribute	Value
Name	Check Parent Level
Type	PL/SQL Function Body (returning Boolean)
PL/SQL Function	Book_Code\Chapter12\Check Parent Level.txt
Error Message	Parent level not found.
When Button Pressed	SAVE

Table 12-18. *Validation: Check Child Level*

Attribute	Value
Name	Check Child Level
Type	PL/SQL Function Body (returning Boolean)
PL/SQL Function	Book_Code\Chapter12\Check Child Level.txt
Error Message	Child account found. Unable to delete account.
When Button Pressed	DELETE

Table 12-19. *Validation: Check in Transaction*

Attribute	Value
Name	Check in Transaction
Type	PL/SQL Function Body (returning Boolean)
PL/SQL Function	Book_Code\Chapter12\Check in Transaction.txt
Error Message	Can't delete. Account has been used in transaction.
When Button Pressed	DELETE

Table 12-20. *Validation: Disallow Code Modification*

Attribute	Value
Name	Disallow Code Modification
Type	PL/SQL Function Body (returning Boolean)
PL/SQL Function	Book_Code\Chapter12\Disallow Code Modification.txt
Error Message	Account code cannot be modified.
When Button Pressed	SAVE
Server-side Condition Type	Item is NOT NULL
Item	P16_ROWID

Each transaction level account (e.g., level 4) must be associated with one of the two specified types: Bank or Others. The validation created in Table 12-21 will prompt users to select one from the specified two types.

Table 12-21. *Validation: Check Account Type*

Attribute	Value
Name	Check Account Type
Type	Item is NOT NULL
Item	P16_COATYPE
Error Message	Please select a Type for the new account.
When Button Pressed	SAVE
Server-side Condition Type	Item = Value
Item	P16_COALEVEL
Value	4

12.7 Modify Process: Process Row of GL_COA

Modify the wizard-generated process (Process Row of GL_COA) as follows:

Table 12-22. *Process: Save Record Attributes*

Attribute	Value
Name	Save Record
Type	PL/SQL Code
PL/SQL Code	Book_Code\Chapter12\Save Record.txt
Sequence	10
Point	Processing
Success Message	Chart of Account record saved.
Error Message	An error occurred while saving COA record.
When Button Pressed	SAVE

12.8 Create Process: Delete Record

The process mentioned in Table 12-23 will delete a COA record after passing all validations.

Table 12-23. *Delete Record Process Attributes*

Attribute	Value
Name	Delete Record
Type	PL/SQL Code
PL/SQL Code	Book_Code\Chapter12\Delete Record.txt
Sequence	20 (*to execute before the Close Dialog and Reset Page processes*)
Point	Processing
Success Message	COA record deleted.
Error Message	An error occurred while deleting COA record.
When Button Pressed	DELETE

12.9 Modify Delete Button

Table 12-24. *Modified Delete Button*

Action	Attribute	Value
Modify Button	Execute Validations	Yes
	Database Action	- Select -

12.10 Modify Save Button

Table 12-25. *Modified Save Button*

Action	Attribute	Value
Modify Button	Label	Save
	Action	Submit Page
	Database Action	-Select-
	Server-side Condition	-Select-

12.11 Delete the Create Button

Delete the Create button from page 16 because the Save button has been enabled to handle both new and modified COA records.

12.12 Create a Highlight Rule

Save your progress and run the module from the Setup ➤ Chart of Accounts menu. Using the Actions menu, create a highlight rule (Actions ➤ Format ➤ Highlight) to highlight the root level, as shown in Figure 12-1. Also, arrange the report columns using the Actions menu in the sequence illustrated in Figure 12-2 (later in the chapter).

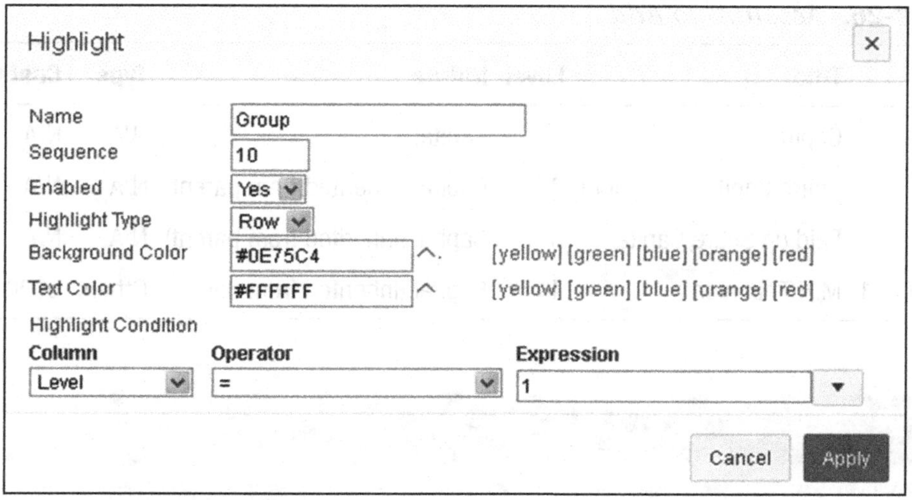

Figure 12-1. *Highlight rule*

12.13 Test Your Work

Click the Create button (on page 15) to add the accounts listed in Table 12-24. Figure 12-2 illustrates the two pages of this module. Note that the level value will be generated automatically for each account. Similarly, the account nature will be inherited by subaccounts from the first level. Use the COA.xls file (located in the Chapter12 folder) to create the complete COA.

Table 12-26. *Accounts to Add*

Code	Title	Level	Nature	Type	Cost Center
1	Capital	1	Capital	N/A	N/A
101	Share Capital & Reserve	2	Capital (Inherited from parent)	N/A	N/A
101001	Paid up Share Capital	3	Capital (Inherited from parent)	N/A	N/A
10100100001	M.H.Thomson	4	Capital (Inherited from parent)	Others	09001

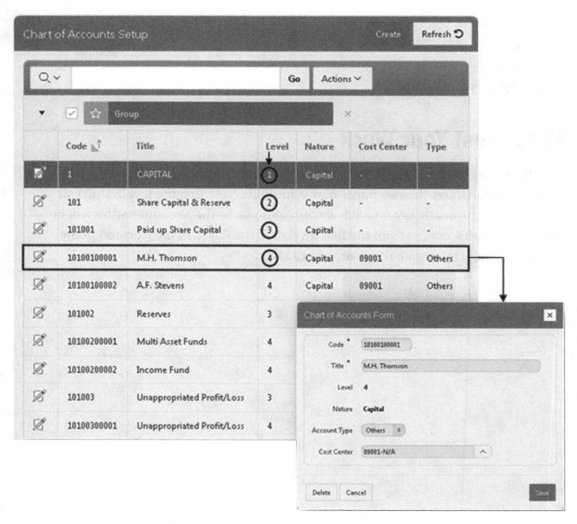

Figure 12-2. *Chart of accounts pages*

12.14 Summary

The chart of accounts setup is the most important segment; without it, you cannot post transactions in the application. It requires ample time to plan, design, and create the COA. Once you create it in this application, you can copy this master COA to other companies to save time. The next chapter will show you how to do that.

CHAPTER 13

Copy Chart of Accounts

As mentioned earlier, the application has the capability of maintaining the accounts of multiple companies simultaneously. To complement this feature, the application contains a utility to allow you to copy the chart of accounts (COA) from one company to another. Obviously, this is a great time-saver when setting up a new company. Before you start development, make sure that the source COA has been created successfully before invoking this utility. The page for this module consists of two select lists. The first allows you to specify the source company whose COA you want to copy from, while the second allows you to select the target company to which you want to copy the source COA.

13.1 Create Page

This segment will be created manually using a blank page. After creating the blank page, you'll add some items and a button to it along with a corresponding process to save a COA for the target company. Create the page and page items as listed in Table 13-1.

© Riaz Ahmed 2019
R. Ahmed, *Cloud Computing Using Oracle Application Express*,
https://doi.org/10.1007/978-1-4842-4243-8_13

Table 13-1. *Page Attributes*

Action	Attribute	Value
Create Page	Page Number	54
	Name	Copy COA
	Page Mode	Normal
	Breadcrumb	—Don't use breadcrumbs on page—
	Navigation Preference	Identify an existing navigation menu entry for this page
	Existing Navigation Menu Entry	Utilities
Create Region	Title	Copy Chart of Accounts
	Type	Static Content
	Template	Standard
Create Page Item	Name	P54_SOURCE
	Type	Popup LOV
	Label	Source Company:
	Region	Copy Chart of Accounts
	Template	Required
	Value Required	Yes
	LOV Type	Shared Component
	Shared Component	COMPANIES
Create Page Item	Name	P54_TARGET
	Type	Popup LOV
	Label	Target Company:
	Region	Copy Chart of Accounts
	Template	Required
	Value Required	Yes
	LOV Type	Shared Component
	Shared Component	COMPANIES

13.2 Add Button

Add a button to the page using Table 13-2. This button will submit the page to run the Copy COA process, covered later in the chapter.

Table 13-2. *Button Attributes*

Action	Attribute	Value
Create Button	Button Name	Copy
	Label	Copy
	Region	Copy Chart of Accounts
	Button Position	Copy
	Hot	Yes
	Action	Submit Page

13.3 Add Validations

The three validations listed in Table 13-3 will ensure that the copy operation is possible.

Table 13-3. *Validation Attributes*

Action	Attribute	Value
Create Validation	Name	Select Different Companies
	Type	PL/SQL Function (returning Error Text)
	PL/SQL Function	Book_Code\Chapter13\Select Different Companies.txt
	When Button Pressed	Copy
Create Validation	Name	Check Source COA
	Type	PL/SQL Function (returning Error Text)
	PL/SQL Function	Book_Code\Chapter13\Check Source COA.txt
	When Button Pressed	Copy
Create Validation	Name	Check Target COA
	Type	PL/SQL Function (returning Error Text)
	PL/SQL Function	Book_Code\Chapter13\Check Target COA.txt
	When Button Pressed	Copy

13.4 Copy COA Process

The process listed in Table 13-4 will copy the source COA to the selected target company, assuming, of course, the previous three validations were successful.

Table 13-4. *Copy COA Process Attributes*

Action	Attribute	Value
Create Process	Name	Copy COA
	Type	PL/SQL Code
	PL/SQL Code	Book_Code\Chapter13\Copy COA.txt
	Point	Processing
	Success Message	Chart of Accounts copied successfully.
	Error Message	Could not copy Chart of Accounts.
	When Button Pressed	Copy

13.5 Test Your Work

Testing of this segment is simple. Invoke this module from the Copy Chart of Accounts option under the Utilities menu. You will see a small form illustrated in Figure 13-1. Select a company from the source LOV whose COA already exists in the database and then attempt to copy it to a company that does not have a COA. The selected company's COA should be copied to the target company followed by the success message. Click the button again and see what happens. It should, of course, fail this time.

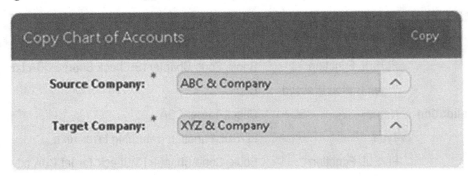

Figure 13-1. *Simple form*

13.6 Summary

After creating the COA for both companies, now you are in a position to post financial transaction through vouchers, which is coming next.

CHAPTER 14

Enter Vouchers

This is the segment that you use to enter and record financial transactions. On the initial page of this segment, you select a voucher type, which you created in Chapter 5. The underneath report gets populated with all the vouchers related to the selected type.

Clicking the Create button calls the Voucher Form page, where you create a new voucher for the selected type. The Voucher Form page contains two regions. The Enter Voucher region displays the selected voucher type and three text items to input the voucher number, date, and description. The number item can receive values up to 10 digits, whereas the date should fall in the month being displayed at the top of the page. Add a description of up to 150 characters to describe the transaction. In the Transaction Details region, you enter transactions by selecting the affected accounts from the chart of accounts (COA) and cost centers, and you input the amount involved in the transaction either in the Debit or Credit column. The Reference column is used to save additional information, such as check or invoice numbers. Using the Add Row button, you can record any number of transactions in a single voucher.

VOUCHER TABLES

--S6A-- TRANSACTION MASTER TABLE

```
CREATE TABLE gl_tran_master
(Tran_No NUMBER, Cocode NUMBER CONSTRAINT fk_tran_master1 REFERENCES
gl_company (Cocode) NOT NULL,
Coyear NUMBER(4) NOT NULL, comonthid NUMBER(2) NOT NULL,
vchcode NUMBER CONSTRAINT fk_tran_master2 REFERENCES gl_voucher(vchcode)
NOT NULL,
vchno NUMBER(10) NOT NULL, vchdate DATE NOT NULL,
vchdescription VARCHAR2(150) NOT NULL, createdby VARCHAR2(10) NOT NULL,
createdon DATE NOT NULL,
vchverified VARCHAR2(1) NOT NULL, vchposted VARCHAR2(1) NOT NULL, closing
```

© Riaz Ahmed 2019
R. Ahmed, *Cloud Computing Using Oracle Application Express*,
https://doi.org/10.1007/978-1-4842-4243-8_14

```
NUMBER(1) NOT NULL,
CONSTRAINT pk_tran_master PRIMARY KEY (tran_no),
CONSTRAINT fk_tran_master3 FOREIGN KEY (Cocode,Coyear,Comonthid) REFERENCES
gL_fiscal_year)
```

--S6B-- TRANSACTION DETAILS TABLE

```
CREATE TABLE gl_tran_detail
(Line_No NUMBER, Tran_No NUMBER NOT NULL,
Cocode NUMBER CONSTRAINT fk_tran_detail1 REFERENCES GL_Company (Cocode)
NOT NULL,
coacode VARCHAR2(11) NOT NULL, cccode VARCHAR2(5), vchdescription
VARCHAR2(150) NOT NULL,
vchdr NUMBER(15,2) NOT NULL, vchcr NUMBER(15,2) NOT NULL, vchreference
VARCHAR2(25),
reconciled NUMBER(1) NOT NULL,
CONSTRAINT pk_tran_detail PRIMARY KEY (line_no), CONSTRAINT fk_tran_detail3
FOREIGN KEY (cocode,cccode) REFERENCES GL_Cost_Center, CONSTRAINT fk_tran_
detail4 FOREIGN KEY (cocode,coacode) REFERENCES GL_COA)
```

--ADD FOREIGN KEY

```
ALTER TABLE gl_tran_detail ADD CONSTRAINT fk_tran_detail2 FOREIGN KEY
(TRAN_NO) REFERENCES gl_tran_master(TRAN_NO) ON DELETE CASCADE ENABLE
```

--S6C-- TRANSACTION TABLE SEQUENCE

```
CREATE SEQUENCE gl_tran_master_seq MINVALUE 1 START WITH 1 INCREMENT BY 1
CACHE 20
CREATE SEQUENCE gl_tran_detail_seq MINVALUE 1 START WITH 1 INCREMENT BY 1
CACHE 20
```

--S6D-- TRIGGER TO POPULATE DEFAULT COST CENTER CODE FROM CHART OF ACCOUNTS (IF LEFT NULL IN VOUCHER)

```
CREATE OR REPLACE TRIGGER "tran_detail_get_cost_center" BEFORE INSERT OR
UPDATE ON gl_tran_detail
FOR EACH ROW
DECLARE
```

```
    Vcccode varchar2(5);
BEGIN
  if :new.cccode is null then
    select cccode into Vcccode from GL_COA where cocode = :new.cocode and
    coacode = :new.coacode;
    :new.cccode := Vcccode;
  end if;
END;

ALTER TRIGGER "TRAN_DETAIL_GET_COST_CENTER" ENABLE
```

Transaction data will be saved in two tables: GL_TRAN_MASTER and GL_TRAN_DETAIL. The master table contains header information for each voucher, while the details table carries transaction information. The two tables are linked together using a common key (TRAN_NO), following a one-to-many relationship in which a single voucher record in the master table can have multiple records in the details table. The tran_detail_get_cost_center trigger is used to populate default cost centers in the details table from the COA when no cost center is selected during voucher creation.

14.1 Create List of Values

Using Table 14-1, create two dynamic lists of values (LOVs) from scratch. You'll use the first LOV in the Transaction Details region to select financial accounts from the COA for each transaction. The second LOV will be used to fetch and create vouchers for the selected type.

Table 14-1. *Dynamic LOVs*

LOV	Query
COA Entry Level	SELECT coacode||'-'||coatitle d, coacode r FROM gl_coa WHERE coalevel=4 and cocode=(select cocode from gl_users where userid = :APP_USER) ORDER BY coacode
Voucher Types	SELECT vchtype d, vchcode r FROM gl_voucher ORDER BY vchtype

14.2 Create Pages

This segment will also comprise two pages, but here you will use the Form ➤ Two Page Master Detail option. The master page (page 42) will show header information from the master table, while the detail page (page 43) will have two regions: Enter Voucher and Transaction Details. The Enter Voucher region will receive header information, whereas the second region will be used to enter details of each transaction. Create the two pages using Table 14-2.

Table 14-2. *Page Attributes*

Wizard Screen	Attribute	Value
Page Attributes	Master Page Number	42
	Master Page Name	Vouchers
	Detail Page Number	43
	Detail Page Name	Voucher Details
Navigation Menu	Navigation Preference	Identify an existing navigation menu entry for this page.
	Existing Navigation Menu Entry	Transactions
Master Source	Table/View Name	GL_TRAN_MASTER
	Primary Key Column	TRAN_NO
	Form Navigation Order	TRAN_NO
	Select Columns	Select all columns from the table
Detail Source	Table/View Name	GL_TRAN_DETAIL
	Primary Key Column	LINE_NO
	Form Navigation Order	TRAN_NO > TRAN_NO
	Select Columns	Select all columns from the table

14.3 Modify the Master Page (Page 42)

Click the Vouchers Interactive Grid region and execute the following steps:

1. Replace the existing SQL query with the one that follows. When
    you select a voucher type from the select list (created in the next
    section), the report is refreshed using the conditions specified
    in the WHERE clause and displays vouchers related to the selected
    company, year, month, and type.

```
SELECT
            "GL_TRAN_MASTER"."TRAN_NO" "TRAN_NO",
            "GL_TRAN_MASTER"."COCODE" "COCODE",
            "GL_TRAN_MASTER"."COYEAR" "COYEAR",
            "GL_TRAN_MASTER"."COMONTHID"
            "COMONTHID",
            "GL_TRAN_MASTER"."VCHCODE" "VCHCODE",
            "GL_TRAN_MASTER"."VCHNO" "VCHNO",
            "GL_TRAN_MASTER"."VCHDATE" "VCHDATE",
            "GL_TRAN_MASTER"."VCHDESCRIPTION"
            "VCHDESCRIPTION",
            "GL_TRAN_MASTER"."CREATEDBY"
            "CREATEDBY",
            "GL_TRAN_MASTER"."CREATEDON"
            "CREATEDON",
            "GL_TRAN_MASTER"."VCHVERIFIED"
            "VCHVERIFIED",
            "GL_TRAN_MASTER"."VCHPOSTED"
            "VCHPOSTED",
            "GL_TRAN_MASTER"."CLOSING" "CLOSING"
FROM "GL_TRAN_MASTER"
WHERE (("GL_TRAN_MASTER"."COCODE" = :P42_COCODE and
"GL_TRAN_MASTER"."COYEAR" = :P42_COYEAR and
            "GL_TRAN_MASTER"."COMONTHID"
            = :P42_COMONTHID and "GL_TRAN_
            MASTER"."VCHCODE" = :P42_VCHCODE))
```

2. Expand the Columns node under the Vouchers region. Using drag and drop to arrange the report columns in this order: TRAN_NO, VCHVERIFIED, VCHPOSTED, VCHNO, VCHDATE, and VCHDESCRIPTION. Also, set the appropriate column headings (shown later in the chapter).

3. Set the Type attribute to Hidden for the COCODE, COYEAR, COMONTHID, VCHCODE, CREATEDBY, CREATEDON, and CLOSING columns.

14.4 Add Items (Page 42)

Using Table 14-3, create three hidden items on the master page to hold the company code, year, and month ID values. You fetch values for these items through individual SELECT statements. These values are forwarded through the Create button to the details page (page 43) to record vouchers in the proper company and period. The Select List item (P42_VCHCODE, listed last in Table 14-3) is added to display all voucher types. When you switch voucher types, the page is submitted to fetch vouchers related to the selected type.

Table 14-3. *Hidden Item Attributes*

Action	Attribute	Value
Create Page Item	Name	P42_COCODE
	Type	Hidden
	Value Protected	Yes (default)
	Region	Vouchers
	Source Type	SQL Query (return single value)
	SQL Query	SELECT cocode FROM gl_users WHERE userid = :app_user
	Source Used	Always, replacing any existing value in session state

(continued)

Table 14-3. (*continued*)

Action	Attribute	Value
Create Page Item	Name	P42_COYEAR
	Type	Hidden
	Value Protected	Yes (default)
	Region	Vouchers
	Source Type	SQL Query (return single value)
	SQL Query	SELECT coyear FROM gl_users WHERE userid = :app_user
	Source Used	Always, replacing any existing value in session state
Create Page Item	Name	P42_COMONTHID
	Type	Hidden
	Value Protected	Yes (default)
	Region	Vouchers
	Source Type	SQL Query (return single value)
	SQL Query	SELECT comonthid FROM gl_users WHERE userid = :app_user
	Source Used	Always, replacing any existing value in session state
Create Page Item	Name	P42_VCHCODE
	Type	Select List
	Label	Select Voucher Type:
	Page Action on Selection	Submit Page (page is refreshed with vouchers of the selected type)
	Region	Vouchers
	Template	Optional
	Label Column Span	2
	LOV Type	Shared Component
	List of Values	VOUCHER TYPES

14.5 Modify Button (Page 42)

Modify the Create button on the master page. Set the Button Position attribute to Copy. In the Behavior section, click the Target attribute link. In the Link Builder dialog box, set the items as illustrated in Figure 14-1. Upon page submission, item values on the master page (preceded with the & symbol and terminated with a full stop) will be forwarded to the corresponding items on page 43 (specified under the Set Items column).

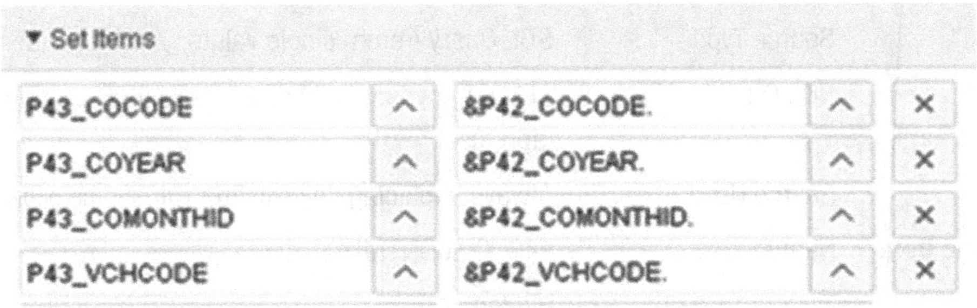

▼ Set Items			
P43_COCODE	∧	&P42_COCODE.	∧ ✕
P43_COYEAR	∧	&P42_COYEAR.	∧ ✕
P43_COMONTHID	∧	&P42_COMONTHID.	∧ ✕
P43_VCHCODE	∧	&P42_VCHCODE.	∧ ✕

Figure 14-1. *Link Builder dialog box*

14.6 Modify the Detail Page (Page 43)

Click the Voucher Details Static Content region (at the top) and set its Title to Enter Voucher; similarly change the title of Voucher Details Interactive Grid region (at the bottom of the page) to Transaction Details. Also, enter VOUCHER in the Static ID attribute of Transaction Details region. This value will be used in a JavaScript in a subsequent section.

Execute the following set of steps to modify the details page:

1. Click the Transaction Details Interactive Grid region and remove the default condition by setting Server-side Condition Type to –Select–. This Interactive Grid was displayed only when P43_TRAN_NO carried some value. With this amendment, the form will always be visible.

2. In the Enter Voucher region, mark all items as Hidden except VCHNO, VCHDATE, and VCHDESCRIPTION. Add appropriate labels (Number, Date, and Description) to the three visible items. Also, set Template to Required, and set Value Required to Yes for

these three items. These three items will accept voucher header information manually from users. All other items will have autogenerated values, as configured in the next couple of steps.

3. Set Default Type to PL/SQL Expression and PL/SQL Expression to V('APP_USER') for P43_CREATEDBY.

4. Set Default Type to PL/SQL Expression and PL/SQL Expression to SYSDATE for P43_CREATEDON.

5. Set Default Type to Static Value and Static Value to N, N, and 0 for P43_VCHVERIFIED, P43_VCHPOSTED, and P43_CLOSING, respectively.

6. Change the Type attribute of P43_VCHDESCRIPTION from Text Field to Textarea. Also, set Label Column Span to 2, Width to 130, Height to 2, and Maximum Length to 150.

7. In the Transaction Details region, set the Type attribute to Hidden for the COCODE and RECONCILED columns.

8. Modify the COCODE column. In the Default section, set its Type to Item and enter **P43_COCODE** in the Item attribute. Note that the database table GL_TRAN_DETAIL has a column labeled COCODE, which is added to the table to implement a constraint. This column will default to the value held in P43_COCODE, which was evaluated and forwarded by the master page in the previous section.

9. Modify the COACODE column. Switch its Type property from Text Field to Popup LOV. Set LOV Type to Shared Component, select COA ENTRY LEVEL for the LOV, and set Width to 35. These changes will present the column as a Popup LOV, from where you can pick an account from the chart of accounts.

10. Modify the CCCODE column. Switch its Type property from Text Field to Popup LOV. Set LOV Type to Shared Component, select COST CENTERS for the LOV, and set Width to 12.

11. Modify the columns VCHDR, VCHCR, and RECONCILED. In the Default section, set the Type attribute to PL/SQL Expression

and enter **0** in the PL/SQL Expression box. These settings will
show zero as the default value in the former two columns.
The zero value is stored in the RECONCILED column to mark
every transaction initially as unreconciled. After reconciling a
transaction with the bank (in Chapter 21), these default values will
be replaced with 1.

14.7 Add/Modify Items

Using Table 14-4, add a Display Only item under the Enter Vouchers region on page 43.
It is added to display the selected voucher type. This item is to be placed between the
VCHCODE and VCHNO items. You assess the voucher type using the value held in the
page item P43_VCHCODE, which was forwarded across; see Figure 14-1.

Table 14-4. *Display Only Item Attributes*

Action	Attribute	Value
Create Page Item	Item Name	P43_VCHTYPE
	Type	Display Only
	Label	Voucher Type:
	Sequence	55 (*to place it properly after the vchcode item*)
	Region	Enter Voucher
	Template	Optional
	Label Column Span	2
	Source Type	SQL Query (return single value)
	SQL Query	SELECT vchtype FROM gl_voucher WHERE vchcode=:P43_VCHCODE
	Source Used	Always, replacing any existing value in session state

The attributes specified in Table 14-5 are set to align the P43_VCHNO and P43_ VCHDATE items horizontally with the Voucher Type item.

Table 14-5. *Alignment Attributes*

Action	Attribute	Value
Modify Item	Item Name	P43_VCHNO
	Start New Row	No
	Label Column Span	2
	Template	Required
	Width	10
	Value Required	Yes
	Maximum Length	10
Modify Item	Item Name	P43_VCHDATE
	Start New Row	No
	Label Column Span	2
	Width	11 (*to hold 01-AUG-2015 format*)
	Maximum Length	11

14.8 Modify Validations on Page 43

Using Table 14-6, modify the 10 default validations. Currently, these validations do not respond to the CREATE button when you create a new voucher.

Table 14-6. *Validation Modifications*

Validations	Attribute	Value
COCODE not null	PL/SQL Expression	**:request in ('SAVE', '<u>CREATE</u>')** or :request like 'GET_NEXT%' or :request like 'GET_PREV%'
COCODE must be numeric		
COACODE not null		
VCHDESCRIPTION not null		
VCHDR not null		
VCHDR must be numeric		
VCHCR not null		
VCHCR must be numeric		
RECONCILED not null		
RECONCILED must be numeric		

14.9 Add Page Items to Show Totals

In this section you will create three page items to show grand totals of Debit and Credit columns. The third page item will be used to show the difference between the first two page items.

Table 14-7. *Create Region to Hold These Page Items*

Action	Attribute	Value
Create Region	Title	Totals
	Type	Static Content
	Parent Region	Transaction Details
	Template	Blank with Attributes

Table 14-8. *Create Page Items*

Action	Attribute	Value
Create First Page Item	Name	P43_TOTDR
	Type	Display Only
	Label	Total Debit
	Save Session State	No
	Region	Totals
	Template	Optional
	Source Type	Null
	Default Type	PL/SQL Expression
	PL/SQL Expression	0
Create Second Page Item	Name	P43_TOTCR
	Type	Display Only
	Label	Total Credit
	Save Session State	No
	Region	Totals
	Start New Row	No
	Template	Optional
	Source Type	Null
	Default Type	PL/SQL Expression
	PL/SQL Expression	0

(*continued*)

Table 14-8. (*continued*)

Action	Attribute	Value
Create Third Page Item	Name	P43_DIFF
	Type	Number Field
	Label	Difference
	Region	Totals
	Start New Row	No
	Template	Optional
	Source Type	Null
	Default Type	Static Value
	Static Value	0

14.10 Add JavaScript to Evaluate Difference

Execute the following step to evaluate difference in a voucher. For this purpose, you need to add a little JavaScript code to page 43.

1. Click the root node (**Page 46: Voucher Details**). Scroll down to **Function and Global Variable Declaration** section and append the code provided in **Book_Code\Chapter14\CalcDiff.txt** just after the existing code in this attribute.

14.11 Create Dynamic Actions

Create the following dynamic actions to calculate the values in Debit and Credit columns and check the difference between these values. The first DA will fire when you modify values in an existing voucher, while the second one will trigger for new vouchers.

Table 14-9. *Create Check Difference (Modify) Dynamic Action*

Action	Attribute	Value
Create Dynamic Action	Name	Check Difference (Modify)
	Event	Click
	Selection Type	Button
	Button	SAVE
	True Action	Execute JavaScript Code
	Code	calcDIFF()

Table 14-10. *Create Check Difference (New) Dynamic Action*

Action	Attribute	Value
Create Dynamic Action	Name	Check Difference (New)
	Event	Click
	Selection Type	Button
	Button	CREATE
	True Action	Execute JavaScript Code
	Code	calcDIFF()

Table 14-11. *Create Check Difference (Before Validation)*
Dynamic Action

Action	Attribute	Value
Create Dynamic Action	Name	Check Difference (Before Validation)
	Event	Before Page Submit
	True Action	Execute JavaScript Code
	Code	calcDIFF()

Table 14-12. *Create Calculate Totals Dynamic Action*

Action	Attribute	Value
Create Dynamic Action	Name	Calculate Totals
	Event	Selection Change [Interactive Grid]
	Selection Type	Region
	Region	Transaction Details
	True Action	Execute JavaScript Code
	Code	Book_Code\Chapter14\Calculate Totals.txt

Note   After creating the Dynamic Actions, if you see "Defined by Dynamic Action" in the Action property for SAVE or CREATE buttons, set this property to Submit Page.

14.12 Add Validations to Page 43

Using Tables 14-13 to 14-19, add four validations to page 43. The first validation (mentioned in Table 14-13) checks for the existence of a voucher number and the presence of a valid voucher date. You cannot use the same number of the same type in the same company, year, and month. Suppose, for example, you are connected to the ABC & Company with January 2015 as your working period. If you try to create JV 1, which already exists in the database, then the system will prevent you from using the same number for the same voucher type. Of course, you can create this number in another period for the same type. The validation also keeps track of invalid dates. For instance, you cannot create vouchers related to February in the month of January. If this is required, then you need to change your working period. The validation will fire when you click any of the four buttons (Create, Save, Next, or Previous).

Table 14-13. *Validation to Check Voucher Number and Date*

Action	Attribute	Value
Create Validation	Name	Check Voucher Number and Date
	Type	PL/SQL Function (returning Error Text)
	PL/SQL Function	Book_Code\Chapter14\Check Number Date.txt
	Error Message	Invalid voucher number and/or date
	Server-side Condition	PL/SQL Expression
	PL/SQL Expression	:request in ('SAVE','CREATE') or :request Like 'GET_NEXT%' or :request Like 'GET_PREV%'

Table 14-14. *Validation to Check Difference in a Voucher*

Action	Attribute	Value
Create Validation	Name	Check Diff (associated with DA)
	Type	PL/SQL Function (returning Error Text)
	PL/SQL Function	Book_Code\Chapter14\Check Diff.txt
	Server-side Condition	PL/SQL Expression
	PL/SQL Expression	:request in ('SAVE','CREATE') or :request Like 'GET_NEXT%' or :request Like 'GET_PREV%'

Table 14-15. *Validation to Check Debit and Credit Values in a Voucher*

Action	Attribute	Value
Create Validation	Name	Debit/Credit Not Zero
	Editable Region	Transaction Details
	Type	PL/SQL Expression
	PL/SQL Expression	:COACODE is NOT NULL and (to_number(:VCHDR) > 0 or to_number(:VCHCR) > 0)
	Error Message	Either Debit or Credit should have some value

Table 14-16. *Validation to Check Verified and Posted Status of a Voucher*

Action	Attribute	Value
Create Validation	Name	Check Verified and Posted Status
	Type	PL/SQL Expression
	PL/SQL Expression	:P43_VCHVERIFIED='N' and :P43_VCHPOSTED='N'
	Error Message	Can't delete this voucher because it is either verified or posted.
	When Button Pressed	DELETE

14.13 Modify Processes

Amend the default processes using the instructions provided in the following tables. The first one is amended to assign the primary key (populated from a sequence) to the page item P43_TRAN_NO. This is value used in the next section to populate the TRAN_NO column in the Transaction Details table. Without this modification, the values defined in the Transaction Details pane will not be propagated to the Transaction Details table. The second amendment is made to display vouchers related to the selected criteria. In the absence of this clause, all vouchers can be navigated through using the Next and Previous buttons, irrespective of company, year, month, and voucher type. The first two processes (Process Row of GL_TRAN_MASTER and Save Interactive Grid Data) are located on the Processing tab, while the last one (Get Next or Previous Primary Key Value) is located under the Pre-Rendering section in the Rendering tab.

Table 14-17. *Modify Process Row of GL_TRAN_MASTER Process*

Process	Attribute	Value
Process Row of GL_TRAN_MASTER	Return Key Into Item = P43_TRAN_NO while **Sequence** is another attribute and its value is **1** with the text under parantheses.	

Table 14-18. *Modify Process Save Interactive Grid Data*

Process	Attribute	Value
Save Interactive Grid Data	Type	PL/SQL Code
	PL/SQL Code	Book_Code\Chapter14\Save IG Data.txt
	Point	Processing
	Editable Region	Transaction Details
	Execution Scope	For Created and Modified Rows
	Server-side Condition	PL/SQL Expression
	PL/SQL Expression	:request in ('SAVE','CREATE') or :request like 'GET_NEXT%' or :request like 'GET_PREV%'

Table 14-19. *Modify Process Get Next or Previous Primary Key Value*

Process	Attribute	Value
Get Next or Previous or Primary Key Value	Navigation Order Column	TRAN_NO
	Runtime Where Clause	COCODE=:P43_COCODE and COYEAR=:P43_COYEAR and COMONTHID=:P43_COMONTHID and VCHCODE=:P43_VCHCODE

14.14 Control Buttons

As per general accounting standards, verified vouchers (Chapter 16) and system generated closing vouchers (Chapter 24) must not be modified or deleted. Using Table 14-20, amend the default conditions specified for the buttons on page 43 to prevent these actions.

Table 14-20. *Button Modifications*

Action	Attribute	Value
Modify Buttons	Button Names	DELETE, SAVE, and CHANGE
	Server-side Condition	PL/SQL Function Body
	PL/SQL Function Body	Book_Code\Chapter14\Control Buttons.txt
Modify Buttons	Button Name	GET_PREVIOUS_TRAN_NO and GET_NEXT_TRAN_NO
	Server-side Condition	PL/SQL Function Body
	PL/SQL Function Body	Book_Code\Chapter14\Control Navigation Buttons.txt

14.15 Test Your Work

This exercise assumes you have completed all the previous chapters fully and have sufficient sample data entered. For instance, selecting a voucher type is mandatory; therefore, you must have created at least one. Similarly, you must also have created a company, year, and month and created a COA. Once you have all these segments in place, follow the next steps to create your first voucher. This is a payment voucher to pay a creditor (A.B. Enterprises) through a bank (ABN Amro), against their invoice number 78345.

1. Select Transactions from the main menu.

2. Select a voucher type on the master page (in my case, it is BPV [Bank Payment Voucher]). Click the Create button. The selected voucher type will be displayed as a read-only item on the details page.

3. Enter **1** for the voucher number.

4. Select a date from the date picker. The date should fall within the period appearing on the top of this page.

5. Type **Paid to A.B. Enterprises against invoice # 78345** in the Description box.

6. In Transaction Details section, click the LOV button in the Account Code column, and select A.B. Enterprises from the pop-up list.

7. Now copy and paste the description from the main Description box (entered in Step 5) into the current row's Description column.

8. Enter **3000** in the Debit column.

9. Enter **Inv # 78345** in the Reference column.

10. Add one more row using the Add Row button.

11. Select a bank account, such as ABN Amro Bank – 30200300001.

12. Paste the same description again for this row.

13. Enter **3000** in the Credit column. Figure 14-2 shows the completed voucher.

14. Click the Create button to save this voucher.

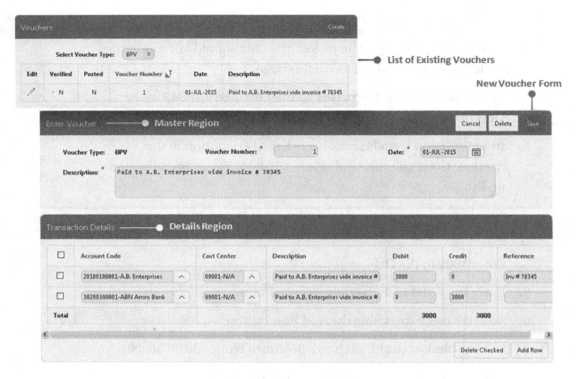

Figure 14-2. *Voucher Master/Detail pages*

14.16 Summary

There are many other things covered in this chapter that need some testing on your part. Revisit these sections and give this segment a thorough test-run by trying different things, especially those related to the four validations. Once you have thoroughly tested the application by entering different types of transactions in different fiscal periods, move on to the next chapter, where you will create a form to search the transactions you entered here.

CHAPTER 15

Search Transactions

The Transaction Search utility helps you locate transactions in a matter of seconds. There are numerous occasions when an accountant needs to search for a specific financial activity entered into a ledger. For example, the accountant may want to know the details of a payment made against invoice number 78345. In this chapter, you will create a search utility to locate a transaction. To search for transactions, a criteria list is provided along with a search box. You select a value from the criteria list (e.g., Reference), then enter a value in the Search box (e.g., **78345**), and finally hit the Search button. The utility searches for the provided value in the selected column and displays the matching records in an interactive report.

15.1 Create Page and Parameters Region

This segment will again be created manually using a blank page, followed by the addition of some page components. It will be invoked from the Utilities menu. Create the page and its components using Table 15-1.

© Riaz Ahmed 2019
R. Ahmed, *Cloud Computing Using Oracle Application Express*,
https://doi.org/10.1007/978-1-4842-4243-8_15

Table 15-1. *Page and Component Attributes*

Action	Attribute	Value
Create BlankPage	Page Number	53
	Name	Search Transaction
	Page Mode	Normal
	Breadcrumb	—Do not use breadcrumbs on page—
	Navigation Preference	Identify an existing navigation menu entry for this page.
	Existing Navigation Menu Entry	Utilities
Create Region	Title	Search Parameters
	Type	Static Content
	Template	Standard
Create Button	Button Name	Search
	Label	Search
	Region	Search Parameters
	Button Position	Copy
	Hot	Yes
	Action	Submit Page
Create Page Item	Name	P53_CRITERION
	Type	Select List
	Label	Criterion:
	Region	Search Parameters
	Label Column Span	2
	Template	Required
	Value Required	Yes

(continued)

Table 15-1. (*continued*)

Action	Attribute	Value
	Static Values (Make sure that there are no spaces before or after the semicolon character.)	STATIC:Voucher Number;TM. VCHNO, Account Code;TD.COACODE, Account Title;COA.COATITLE, Debit;TD.VCHDR, Credit; D.VCHCR, Master Description;TM. VCHDESCRIPTION, Detail Description;TD. VCHDESCRIPTION, Reference;TD.VCHREFERENCE
Create Page Item	Name	P53_SEARCH
	Type	Text Field
	Label	\Search:\
	Region	Search Parameters
	Start New Row	No
	Label Column Span	2
	Template	Required
	Width	100
	Value Required	Yes

The LOV defined in the select list (P53_CRITERION) has eight options. Each option comprises two values: a display value and a return value. The value placed in the display position is shown to users. When the user selects a value, the return value is what actually gets returned to the program. For example, when the user selects a voucher number from the list, the program will receive a return value of TM.VCHNO, which is the voucher number from the transaction master table. This value is then used in the WHERE clause of the SQL statement covered in the next section to fetch the required records.

15.2 Create an Interactive Report Region

The interactive report region created in Table 15-2 will show all the searched records beneath the parameters region. It is based on a SELECT query that joins multiple tables to provide complete information. The WHERE clause in this statement uses the value returned by the criterion select list via the DECODE function. Note that COATITLE, VCHDESCRIPTION, and VCHREFERENCE are character columns, so values in these columns are searched using the LIKE operator.

***Table 15-2.** Interactive Report Region*

Action	Attribute	Value
Create Region	Title	Search Result
	Type	Interactive Report
	Type (under Source)	SQL Query
	SQL Query	SELECT TM.TRAN_NO, TM.VCHDATE, VCH.VCHTYPE, TM.VCHNO, TD.COACODE, COA.COATITLE, TM.VCHDESCRIPTION MD, TD.VCHDESCRIPTION DD, TD.VCHDR, TD.VCHCR, TD.VCHREFERENCE FROM GL_COA COA, GL_VOUCHER VCH, GL_TRAN_MASTER TM, GL_TRAN_DETAIL TD WHERE TM.COCODE=TD.COCODE AND TM.COCODE= COA.COCODE AND TM.TRAN_NO=TD.TRAN_NO AND TM.VCHCODE=VCH.VCHCODE AND TD.COACODE= COA.COACODE AND TM.COCODE=(select cocode from gl_users where userid=:APP_USER)

(*continued*)

Table 15-2. (*continued*)

Action	Attribute	Value
		AND
		(
		decode(: P53_CRITERION,'TD.COACODE',TD. COACODE)=:P53_SEARCH
		OR decode(: P53_CRITERION,'COA.COATITLE',upper (COA.COATITLE)) **Like** upper(:P53_SEARCH)
		OR decode(: P53_CRITERION,'TD.VCHCR',TD. VCHCR)=:P53_SEARCH
		OR decode(: P53_CRITERION,'TD.VCHDR',TD. VCHDR)=:P53_SEARCH
		OR decode(: P53_CRITERION,'TD. VCHDESCRIPTION',upper(TD. VCHDESCRIPTION)) **Like** upper(:P53_SEARCH)
		OR decode(: P53_CRITERION,'TM.VCHDESCRIPTION', upper(TM.VCHDESCRIPTION)) **Like** upper(:P53_SEARCH)
		OR decode(: P53_CRITERION,'TD.VCHREFERENCE', upper(TD.VCHREFERENCE)) **Like** upper(:P53_SEARCH)
		OR decode(: P53_CRITERION,'TM.VCHNO',TM. VCHNO)=:P53_SEARCH)
		)
		ORDER BY TM.VCHDATE
	Template	Standard

Add meaningful column headings (as shown later in the chapter in Figure 15-1) to the report by expanding the Columns node under the Search Result interactive report.

15.3 Add a Dynamic Action

Using Tables 15-3 and 15-4, add a dynamic action to enable a wildcard character (%) to be used to allow the searching of values in character columns. The true action fires when you select a criterion from the list. The dynamic action then places the text *%put search string between these symbols%* into the search box (P53_SEARCH) to inform users that the character search should be added in between the two percent signs. The false action (in other words, when a numeric criterion is selected) makes the search box empty. The two parameter values (criterion and searched value) are then used in the WHERE clause (in the previous section) to filter records in the SELECT statement.

Table 15-3. *Dynamic Action For Static Assignment*

Action	Attribute	Value
Create Dynamic Action	Name	Put Percent Sign
	Event	Change
	Selection Type	Item(s)
	Item(s)	P53_CRITERION
	Client-side Condition	Item is in list
	List	COA.COATITLE, TM.VCHDESCRIPTION, TD.VCHDESCRIPTION, TD.VCHREFERENCE
	Action (under Show)	Set Value
	Set Type	Static Assignment
	Value	%put search string between these symbols%
	Item (Under Affected Elements)	P53_SEARCH

Right-click the False node, and select Create False Action. Set the attributes in Table 15-4 for the False action.

Table 15-4. *False Action Attributes*

Attribute	Value
Action	Set Value
Set Type	Static Assignment
Value	*Leave Blank*
Selection Type	Item(s)
Item(s)	P53_SEARCH

15.4 Test Your Work

Invoke this page from the Utilities menu's Search Transaction option, and execute the following steps to search a transaction that you recorded in the Chapter 14:

1. Select Reference from the Criterion list. The search box will prompt you to enter a value within % symbols. Do so by entering **78345** between these symbols and hit the Search button. You'll get the voucher information you entered in the Chapter 14, as illustrated in Figure 15-1.

2. Switch criterion to Debit. Enter **3000** in the Search box, and click the Search button. Once again, the same record appears on your screen, but this time it is fetched using numeric parameters.

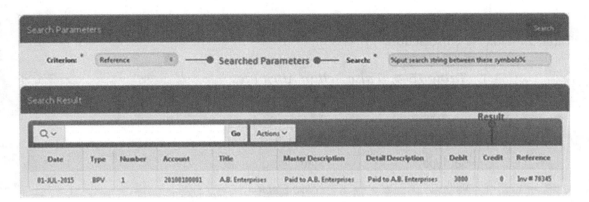

Figure 15-1. *Search results*

15.5 Summary

Once your data piles up in the database, the Search Transaction utility helps you dig out a financial event from the data mine. In the next chapter, you will create a segment that protects data from manipulation.

CHAPTER 16

Vouchers Verification

The Vouchers Verification segment serves two purposes. First, it allows authorized staff to check the accuracy of business transactions, and second, it prevents verified vouchers from being modified or deleted. Its main interface provides a Parameters region, where you enter a range of dates and specify whether you want to see Unverified or Verified vouchers. The date parameters receive voucher creation dates (not the voucher date). The lower region of the page displays a list of vouchers based on the selected criteria. Each voucher's detail record starts with a link column, which calls another page where an authorized person can see a complete voucher with all its details. The page carries appropriate buttons to verify/unverify the voucher being shown.

16.1 Create Page and Parameters Region

Create a blank page and configure it using Table 16-1.

Table 16-1. *Page Attributes and Parameters Region*

Action	Attribute	Value
Create Blank Page	Page Number	94
	Name	Vouchers Verification
	Page Mode	Normal
	Breadcrumb	—Do not use breadcrumbs on page—
	Navigation Preference	Identify an existing navigation menu entry for this page
	Existing Navigation Menu Entry	Closing

(continued)

© Riaz Ahmed 2019
R. Ahmed, *Cloud Computing Using Oracle Application Express*,
https://doi.org/10.1007/978-1-4842-4243-8_16

Table 16-1. (*continued*)

Action	Attribute	Value
Create Region	Title	Parameters
	Type	Static Content
	Template	Standard
Create Page Item	Name	P94_FROM
	Type	Date Picker
	Label	\From\
	Region	Parameters
	Label Column Span	2
	Template	Required
	Value Required	Yes
	Source Type	PL/SQL Expression
	Item Source Value	SYSDATE
Create Page Item	Name	P94_TO
	Type	Date Picker
	Label	\To\
	Region	Parameters
	Label Column Span	2
	Template	Required
	Value Required	Yes
	Source Type	PL/SQL Expression
	Item Source Value	SYSDATE
Create Page Item	Name	P94_CRITERION
	Type	Radio Group
	Label	\Select:\
	Number of Columns	2
	Region	Parameters

(*continued*)

Table 16-1. (*continued*)

Action	Attribute	Value
	Label Column Span	2
	LOV Type	Static Values
	Template	Optional
	Static Values	STATIC:Unverified;N,Verified;Y
	Display Null Value	No
	Default Type	Static Value
	Static Value	N
Create Button	Button Name	Get
	Label	Get
	Region	Parameters
	Button Position	Copy
	Hot	Yes
	Action	Submit Page

The two date picker items are added to the page where users will specify a range of voucher creation dates. The purpose of using the Created On date column is to make it easier for the verifying person to call all vouchers entered on a specific date, irrespective of the financial period. For example, if the authorized person verifies all vouchers on a daily basis, then that person will need to view a list of all vouchers created today. The radio group item is added to filter vouchers according to the selected criterion: Unverified or Verified. Once a voucher is marked as Verified, it vanishes from the Unverified list and can be seen only by selecting the Verified option.

16.2 Create Interactive Report Region

The interactive report region in Table 16-2 is based on a SELECT statement. The region refreshes when a user clicks the Get button after choosing one option from the radio group. Note that this report is based on the CREATEDON column, which means that the user will have to put a voucher creation date, not the voucher date itself, in the two date boxes. For example, a voucher dated 01-JAN-2015 is created on January 2, 2015, and can be viewed in this report only when you enter **02-JAN-2015** in the date boxes. The Closing column in the transaction master table is a tag that is used by the application to identify year-end vouchers. A value of 1 in this column signifies that the voucher is a system-generated closing voucher and is not user-modifiable. See Chapter 29 for more on closing vouchers.

Table 16-2. *Interactive Report Region Attributes*

Action	Attribute	Value
Create Region	Title	Vouchers Verification
	Type	Interactive Report
	Type (under Source)	SQL Query
	SQL Query	SELECT * FROM gl_tran_master WHERE cocode=(select cocode from gl_users where Userid = :APP_USER) AND **createdon** between :P94_FROM AND :P94_TO AND vchverified=:P94_CRITERION AND **closing**=0 ORDER BY vchdate
	Template	Standard

After creating the region, amend the interactive report region as follows:

1. Hide all columns except VCHNO, VCHDATE, VCHDESCRIPTION, CREATEDBY, and CREATEDON. Also add the appropriate headings to these visible columns, as shown in Figure 16-1 later in the chapter.

2. Create a link in the TRAN_NO column. This link will open page 95 to display the selected voucher, where you can mark it as verified and can even reverse it. The Set Items section is populated with some key values that are passed to the verification page for further processing. Recall that for page 42 (Vouchers), you created three hidden items (P42_COCODE, P42_COYEAR, and P42_COMONTHID) and stored the appropriate values in these items through SQL statements for this purpose. You didn't do

this for page 94 because on page 42 hidden items were created
to add conditions to the wizard- generated report query. Here,
you do not need these items, as you have already placed filters
in the WHERE clause of the interactive report's SQL query. The
items (P95_COCODE, P95_COYEAR, P95_COMONTHID, and
P95_VCHCODE) on page 95 (coming up next) are populated with
values from the interactive report items: &P94_COCODE., &P94_
COYEAR., &P94_COMONTHID., and &P94_VCHCODE. Set the
attributes mentioned in Table 16-3 to create the link.

Table 16-3. *Link Attributes*

Action	Attribute	Value	
Modify Column	Column Name	TRAN_NO	
	Type	Link	
	Heading	Call	
	Column Alignment	Center	
	Target	Type = Page In This Application	
		Page = 95	
		Set Items	
		Name	**Value**
		P95_TRAN_NO	#TRAN_NO#
		P95_COCODE	&P94_COCODE.
		P95_COYEAR	&P94_COYEAR.
		P95_COMONTHID	&P94_COMONTHID.
		P95_VCHCODE	&P94_VCHCODE.
		Clear Cache = 95	
	Link Text	<img src="#IMAGE_PREFIX#app_ui/img/icons/apex-editview.png" class="apex-edit-view" alt="">	

16.3 Create Verification Page

The main vouchers verification page will be created from the Voucher Details page you created in Chapter 14. Edit page 43, click the Create menu ⊞∨, and select the option Page as Copy. Follow the wizard and set the attributes listed in Table 16-4.

Table 16-4. *Verification Page Attributes*

Attribute	Value
Create a page as a copy of	Page in this application
Copy from Page	43. Voucher Details
New Page Number	95
New Page Name	Vouchers Verification Page
Breadcrumb	—Do not use breadcrumbs on page—
New Names Page	*Accept all the default new values*
Navigation Preference	Identify an existing navigation menu entry for this page.
Existing Navigation Menu Entry	Closing

A copy of the Voucher Details page is created with a new ID (page 95). The new page will function just like the one it is copied from. Let's modify it to restrict some of its functions and add some new components so that it can perform the intended task of verification.

16.4 Modify, Delete, and Create Page Buttons

The first amendment mentioned in Table 16-5 is being made on page 95 to handle the application flow when the Cancel button is clicked. When clicked, this button will turn the flow back to page 94 instead of page 42.

Table 16-5. *Cancel Button Attributes*

Action	Attribute	Value
Modify Button	Button Name	CANCEL
	Target Page	94

Delete the five buttons mentioned in Table 16-6 because they are no longer applicable to this segment.

Table 16-6. *Button Deletions*

Action	Attribute	Value
Delete Buttons	Button Name	DELETE, SAVE, CREATE

Now add two new buttons, as listed in Table 16-7. The first button will be displayed for vouchers that are yet to be verified (P95_VCHVERIFIED=N), while the second one will appear for those vouchers that are already marked as verified.

Table 16-7. *New Buttons Attributes*

Action	Attribute	Value Button 1	Value Button 2
Create Buttons	Button Name	Verify	Unverify
	Label	Verify	Unverify
	Region	Enter Voucher	Enter Voucher
	Button Position	Copy	Copy
	Hot	Yes	Yes
	Action	Submit Page	Submit Page
	Server-side Condition	Item = Value	Item = Value
	Item	P95_VCHVERIFIED	P95_VCHVERIFIED
	Value	N	Y

> **Tip**   To set the same attribute value for multiple page items, select all items using Ctrl+click and set the desired value.

16.5 Modify Page-Rendering Process

On the Rendering tab, expand the Pre-Rendering node and click the process named Get Next or Previous Primary Key Value. Replace its existing Runtime Where clause using Table 16-8 to fetch and display vouchers according to the specified criteria.

Table 16-8. *Modify Page-Rendering Process*

Action	Attribute	Value
Modify	Name	Get Next or Previous Primary Key Value
Process	Runtime Where Clause	COCODE=:P95_COCODE and createdon between :P94_FROM and :P94_TO and vchverified=:P94_CRITERION and CLOSING=0

16.6 Delete Validations

Delete all validations from this page. Since all the validations on this page relate to the voucher entry segment, they are not applicable to the verification process.

16.7 Delete Processes

Just like validations, you do not need the defined six processes for this segment. So, delete all these processes.

16.8 Add Processes

Using Table 16-9, add two processes. As the name implies, the first process (Verify) marks a voucher as verified in the transaction master table. The second one is just the opposite and is added to reverse the verification process. Once a voucher is marked as verified, normal users cannot amend or delete it unless an authorized person reverses its state to unverified. Note that since each transaction number (TRAN_NO) is generated uniquely and belongs to a particular company, no more comparisons are needed in the UPDATE statement's WHERE clause.

Table 16-9. *Process Attributes*

Action	Attribute	Value
Create Process	Name	Verify
	Type	PL/SQL Code
	PL/SQL Code	update gl_tran_master set vchverified='Y' where tran_no=:P95_TRAN_NO;
	Point	Processing
	When Button Pressed	Verify
Create Process	Name	Unverify
	Type	PL/SQL Code
	PL/SQL Code	update gl_tran_master set vchverified='N' where tran_no=:P95_TRAN_NO;
	Point	Processing
	When Button Pressed	Unverify

16.9 Handle Branches

Set the following attributes for the three branches:

Table 16-10. *Branch Attributes*

Branch	Attribute	Value
Go To Page 43 (After Submit node)	Name	Go To Page 95
	Target Type	Page in this application
	Page	95
	Name (under Set Items)	P95_TRAN_NO
	Value	&P95_TRAN_NO_NEXT.
Go To Page 43 (After Submit Node)	Name	Go To Page 95
	Target Type	Page in this application
	Page	95
	Name (under Set Items)	P95_TRAN_NO
	Value	&P95_TRAN_NO_PREV.
Go To Page 42 (After Processing Node)	Name	Stay on this page
	Target Type	Page in this application
	Page	95
	Name (under Set Items)	P95_TRAN_NO
	Value	&P95_TRAN_NO_NEXT.
	Server-side Condition	Request is contained in Value
	Value	Verify,Unverify

16.10 Test Your Work

Execute the following steps to test this segment, which you can invoke from the Closing menu:

1. Select a date range in which you entered vouchers (see Figure 16-1).

2. With the Unverified option selected, hit the Get button. The Vouchers Verification region will be populated with all unverified vouchers.

3. Click the Call link for a voucher to bring up page 95 with all the details of the selected voucher.

4. Click the Verify button on this page (that is, page 95). The selected voucher will be marked as verified, and the next voucher will come up automatically for verification.

5. Click the Cancel button. Select the Verified option from the Parameters region and click Get again to have a list of all the vouchers you just verified.

6. Go to Select menu (from the main menu), and select the appropriate period for which you created the previously verified vouchers. Select Transactions from the main menu followed by the type of voucher you just verified. The Verified column on this page should now be displaying Y for all the verified vouchers. Click the Edit link for a verified voucher to open its details. Note that all the buttons, except Cancel and Add Row, have disappeared. This is because of the condition that you implemented in Chapter 14 (see Table 14-13), which says that you can hide all buttons if a voucher either is marked as verified or is an autogenerated closing voucher, which you'll create in Chapter 29.

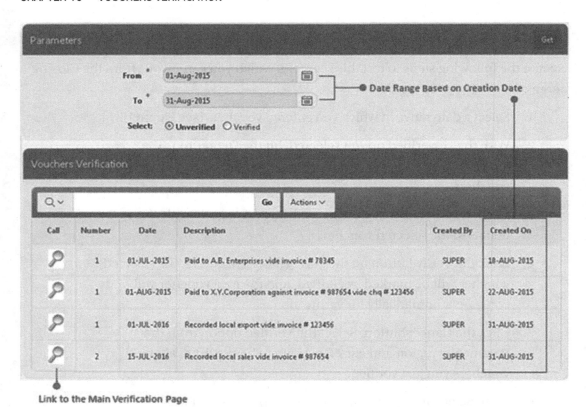

Figure 16-1. *Voucher verification*

16.11 Summary

In this chapter, you created a mechanism that not only ensures the accuracy of transactions but also prevents data manipulation. After verifying a voucher, a user can print its hard copy, which comes next.

CHAPTER 17

Vouchers Report

The application enables you to make hard copies of vouchers. Using this feature you can print either a single voucher or multiple vouchers at once. Note that the output format for all the reports created in this application will be PDF. To get these PDFs, you must have access to a print server, such as Oracle BI Publisher or JasperReport. In this chapter, you will learn how to integrate Jasper Reports in your Apex application that will provide a cost-free alternative for high-fidelity printing in Oracle APEX. For this purpose you will use a free kit known as JasperReportsIntegration kit to run JasperReports reports from within an APEX application.

For this chapter, I assume that you are running Oracle APEX on your own local computer and the reports are stored locally in the file system accessible to the J2EE container (Tomcat 8.5.34) running the JasperReportsIntegration J2EE application (JasperReportsIntegration.war). This application will connect to the desired Oracle schema using connection information deployed in the J2EE container.

17.1 Download and Configure JasperReportsIntegration

1. Download JasperReportsIntegration kit from `http://www.opal-consulting.de/downloads/free_tools/JasperReportsIntegration/2.4.0/`.

2. Extract JasperReportsIntegration-2.4.0.0.zip to **C:\JasperReportsIntegration**.

3. Open a command prompt and change directory to **C:\JasperReportsIntegration\sql**.

4. C:\JasperReportsIntegration\sql>**sqlplus sys as sysdba**

© Riaz Ahmed 2019
R. Ahmed, *Cloud Computing Using Oracle Application Express*,
https://doi.org/10.1007/978-1-4842-4243-8_17

5. SQL>**@sys_install.sql DMS** (Here, DMS is the app schema containing vouchers information.)

6. Exit SQLPLUS.

7. C:\JasperReportsIntegration\sql>**sqlplus DMS/<schema password>**

8. SQL>**@user_install.sql**

17.2 Install Apache Tomcat

1. Download and install JDK. I installed **jdk-7u55-windows-i586**. (http://www.oracle.com/technetwork/java/javase/ downloads/java-archive-downloads-javase7-521261.html).

2. Download and then launch **apache-tomcat-8.5.34.exe** file. I used **32-bit/64-bit Windows Service Installer** for this lab. (Download from https://tomcat.apache.org/download-80.cgi.)

3. On the Configuration screen, set **8888** for *HTTP/1.1 Connector Port*. Enter **admin** in both User Name and Password boxes.

4. After the installation, start Apache Tomcat services using its icon in the system tray.

5. Open browser, type **localhost:8888** in the address bar and hit **Enter**.

6. Click the **manager webapp** link (under Managing Tomcat section) and enter admin/admin for username and password. This will show the Tomcat Web Application Manager page.

7. Close the browser and stop Apache Tomcat services using its icon in the system tray.

8. Copy files **ojdbc6.jar** and **orai18n.jar** from <u>C:\JasperReportsIntegration\lib</u> to <u>C:\Program Files\Apache Software Foundation\Tomcat 8.5\lib</u>.

9. Copy file **JasperReportsIntegration.war** from C:\JasperReportsIntegration\
    webapp to C:\Program Files\Apache Software Foundation\Tomcat 8.5\
    webapps.

10. Restart Apache Tomcat service.

11. From C:\Program Files\Apache Software Foundation\Tomcat8.5\
    webapps\JasperReportsIntegration\WEB-INF\conf folder, open
    application.properties file and set the following parameters:

    [datasource:default]

    type=jdbc

    name=default

    url=jdbc:oracle:thin:@127.0.0.1:1521:XE

    username=DMS

    password=DMS

12. Stop and restart Apache Tomcat service.

17.3 Grant Network Privileges

1. Open a command prompt and switch to
    C:\JasperReportsIntegration\sql.

2. C:\JasperReportsIntegration\sql>**sqlplus sys as sysdba**

3. SQL>**@sys_install_acl.sql DMS** (Here, DMS is the app schema.)

Everything is set. The next move is to create a report and integrate it with Oracle
APEX.

17.4 Creating PDF Reports in Oracle APEX Using JasperReports

After setting up JasperReportsIntegration and Apache Tomcat, you can design reports in Jasper Studio 6.1 and deploy and integrate them with Oracle APEX. Here's a list of steps you need to perform to accomplish the task:

- Download and Install Jasper Studio 6.1. I used **TIBCOJaspersoftStudio-6.1.1.final-windows-installer-x86.exe**. (`https://sourceforge.net/projects/jasperstudio/files/ JaspersoftStudio-6.1.1/`).

- Download Oracle driver for JDBC (ojdbc6.jar), which can be downloaded from `http://www.oracle.com/technetwork/database/ enterprise-edition/jdbc-112010-090769.html`. The file will be utilized in a subsequent section.

- Create a new data source in Jasper Studio 6.1.

- Create your new report with Jasper Studio, compile it, and save it on your computer.

- Copy the compiled file (.jasper) to appropriate location.

- Integrate the report with Oracle APEX and call it from your APEX application via an API.

17.5 Create Database Connection

This exercise assumes that you have downloaded and installed Jasper Studio using its .exe file and have also downloaded ojdbc6.jar file that you need in Step 3. Launch the software and execute the following steps to create a connection to your XE database, which resides on your local machine.

1. Select **File | New | Data Adapter** from the main menu. The first screen of the Data Adapter Wizard will appear, as shown in Figure 17-1. On this screen you will see a folder named MyReports. This is the folder where your data adapter's XML file and reports will be stored. On my PC, this folder is created under: D:\JaspersoftWorkspace. The

XML file contains jdbc data adapter class, name, driver, username, password and other connection information. Enter a meaningful name for the XML file (e.g., GL_ADAPTER.xml) in the *File name* box, and click **Next**.

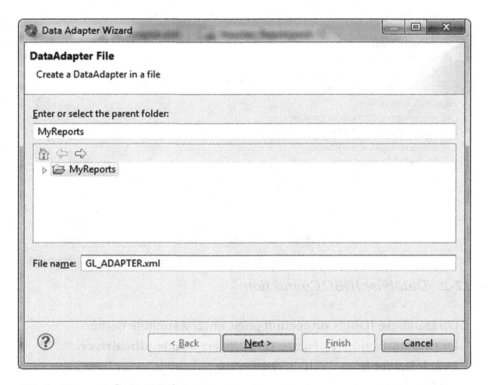

Figure 17-1. *Data Adapter File*

2. On the second wizard screen, select **Database JDBC Connection** (as illustrated in Figure 17-2) and click **Next**.

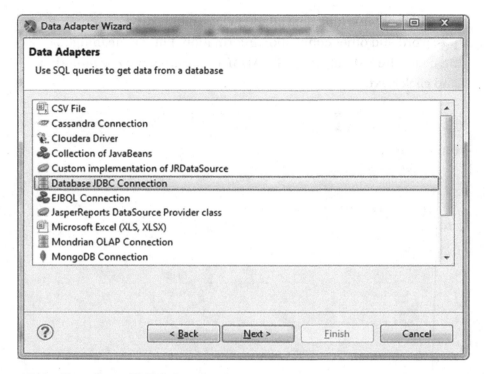

Figure 17-2. *Database JDBC Connection*

3. On Database JDBC Connection page, enter a suitable name
    for the connection (A, Figure 17-3). Select **oracle.jdbc.driver.
    OracleDriver** from the JDBC Driver list (B). Then, enter JDBC
    Url (C). Enter your database username and password in
    corresponding boxes. Click the **Driver Classpath** tab (D), and
    click the **Add** button (E). In the Open dialog box, select the
    ojdbc6.jar file (F) and click **Open**. All these instructions are
    marked in Figure 17-3. On the Database JDBC Connection wizard
    page, click the **Test** button. If everything is okay, you will see a
    dialog box displaying *Successful*. Click **OK** followed by **Finish** to
    complete the connection process. The new connection will appear
    under Data Adapters in the Repository Explorer in the left pane.

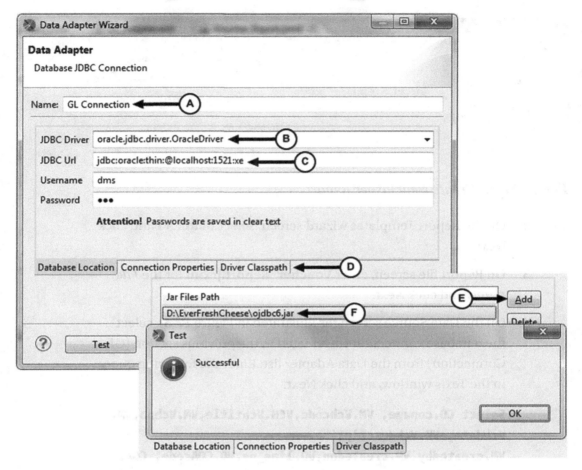

Figure 17-3. *Database JDBC Connection Parameters*

17.6 Create Vouchers Report

Here are the steps to create the vouchers report in Jasper Studio.

17.6.1 Specify Data Source

Execute the following set of steps to specify report's data source and other preliminary parameters:

1.   Select **File | New | Jasper Report** from the main studio menu.

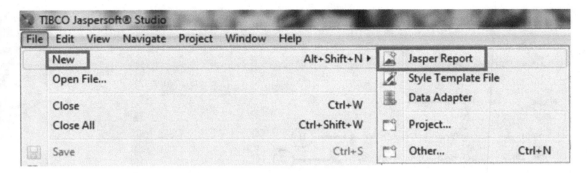

Figure 17-4. *Create New Jasper Report*

2.   On the Report Templates wizard screen, select **Blank A4** and click **Next**.

3.   On Report file screen, enter **Voucher_Report.jrxml** for the *File name*, and click **Next**.

4.   On the Data Source screen (as illustrated in Figure 17-5), select the database connection you created in the previous section (GL Connection) from the Data Adapter list. Enter the following query in the Texts window, and click **Next**.

```
Select CO.coname, VM.Vchcode,VCH.Vchtitle,VM.Vchno,VM.
Vchdate, VM.Vchdescription,
VM.createdby,VM.createdon,VD.line_no,VD.COAcode, COA.
COAtitle,VD.CCCode,CC.CCTitle,
VD.Vchdr,VD.Vchcr,VD.Vchreference,
(SELECT TO_CHAR(SYSDATE, 'DD-MON-YYYY HH24:MI:SS') FROM
DUAL) NOW
From GL_COMPANY CO, GL_VOUCHER VCH, GL_COA COA, GL_COST_
CENTER CC,
GL_TRAN_MASTER VM, GL_TRAN_DETAIL VD
Where VM.cocode=CO.cocode AND VM.tran_no=VD.tran_no AND
            VM.Vchcode=VCH.Vchcode AND VD.cocode=COA.
            cocode AND
            VD.COAcode=COA.COAcode AND VD.CCCode=CC.
            CCCode(+)
ORDER BY VCHCODE,VCHNO,LINE_NO
```

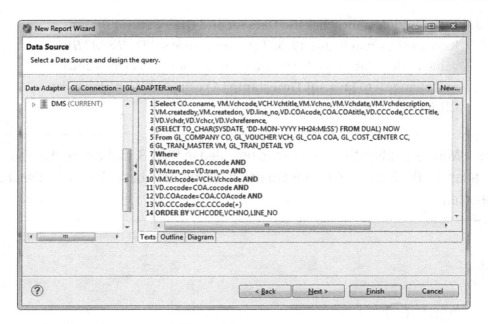

Figure 17-5. *Data Source and Report Query*

5. On Fields screen, click the button symbolized with >> to select all fields, and click **Next**.

6. On Group By screen, move **VCHCODE**, **VCHNO**, and **VCHDATE** columns to the right pane to group the report on these columns. Click **Next**.

7. Click **Finish** to complete the process.

8. In the middle pane, click the **DataSet and Query editor dialog**
    icon, as shown in Figure 17-6. If you see *oracle.sql.TIMESTAMPLTZ*
    value under Class Type for date columns, double-click this entry
    and change it to **java.sql.Timestamp** (A) using the drop-down list.
    Click **OK**.

Note   While executing the instructions provided in Step 8, make sure that the
data adapter (B - Figure 17-6) you created in Create Database Connection section
is selected.

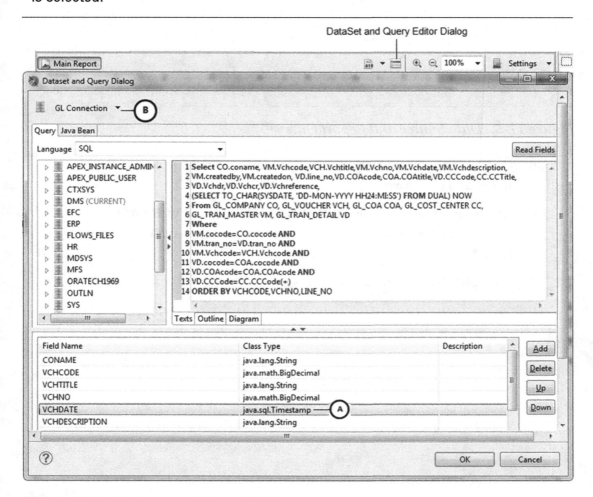

Figure 17-6. *Dataset and Query Dialog*

17.6.2 Designing Report

The vouchers report will be designed in Jasper Studio according to the layout illustrated in Figure 17-7:

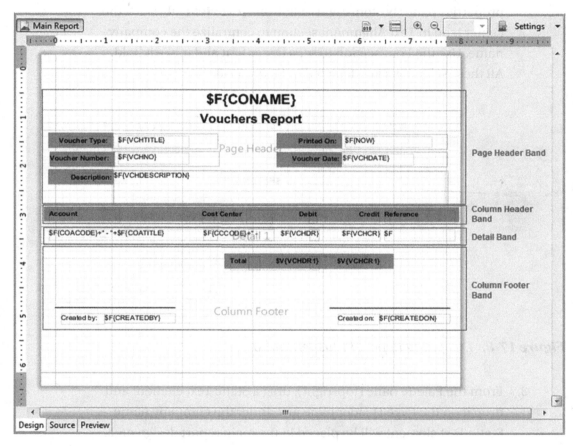

Figure 17-7. *Vouchers Report Layout in JasperStudio*

1. In the Outline pane to your left, right-click **VCHCODE Group Header 1** node and select **Add Band** to add this band to the designer area. Repeat this action for **VCHNO Group Header 1**, and **VCHDATE Group Header 1** nodes as well. In the Main Report designer pane, click the VCHCODE Group Header 1 band, and put a checkmark on the option labeled **Start New Page** that is available in the Appearance tab under the Properties pane on the right side. By turning this property on, each voucher will be printed on a new page. Turn this option on for the other two group headers.

2.   Again, in the Outline pane, expand the Fields node, and drag the **CONAME** field and drop it on the **Page Header** section in the middle pane, as illustrated in Figure 17-8. In the TextField Wizard dialog, select **No Calculation Function** and click **Finish**. In the properties pane (bottom-right), click the **Text Field** tab. Click the center icon in Text Alignment section to centralize the company name. Use the Font section to set a larger font and make it bold. All these selections are depicted in Figure 17-8.

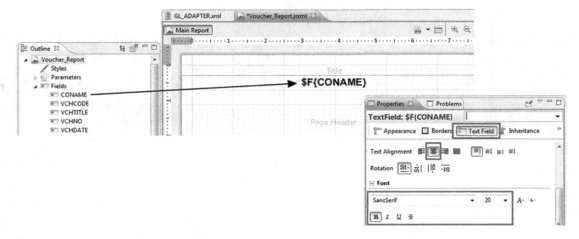

Figure 17-8.   *Designing Report in JasperStudio*

3.   From the Palette pane (top-right), drag a Static Text element and drop it on the Page Header pane just under the company name. A Static Text element will be placed in the main report design area. Double-click this element and type **Vouchers Report**.

4.   Using the instructions provided in Steps 2 and 3, place five static text elements and VCHTITLE, VCHNO, VCHDESCRIPTION, NOW, and VCHDATE fields into the Page Header section, as shown in Figure 17-7.

5.   From the Fields node, drag **COACODE** column and drop it in the Detail 1 section. When you drop a column in the Detail section, the corresponding column name is placed automatically in the Column Header section. Double-click the COACODE header

and set its label to **Account**. In the Detail section, double-click the COACODE column. This will bring up a dialog named Expression Editor. In the expression editor, set expression for this column as **$F{COACODE}+" - "+$F{COATITLE}** to concatenate account code and title values and click **Finish**.

6. Repeat Step 5 to join Cost Center code and title.

7. Click the column $F(CCCODE). Enter **!$F{CCCODE}.equals (" ")** in the **Print When Expression** under Appearance in the Properties pane to suppress printing of null text.

8. Add VCHDR, VCHCR, and VCHREFERENCE column to the Details pane, as shown in Figure 17-7. Click the $F{VCHREFERENCE} column and select the option **Blank When NULL** in the properties pane to suppress null printing.

9. Drag VCHDR column from the Fields node and drop it in the Column Footer section. Select **Sum** from the TexField Wizard dialog to display total for this column at the bottom of each voucher, and click **Finish**. Using Ctrl+Click, select the four VCHDR and VCHCR columns. Click the Pattern property's ellipsis button in the Properties pane. In the Format Pattern dialog box, check the option labeled **Use 1000 separator**, and click **Finish**. The Pattern property can be used to format date columns as well.

10.   Click the Preview tab to see an output similar to Figure 17-9.

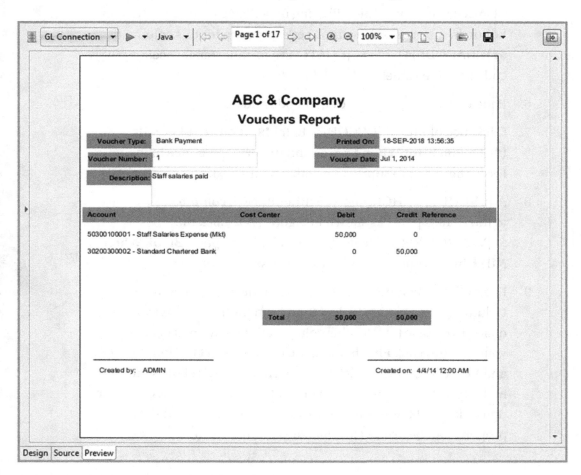

Figure 17-9.   *Voucher Report Final Output*

11.   In the Outline pane, expand the Parameters pane. Right-click the
Parameters node, and select **Create Parameter**. A new parameter
will be added. In the Properties pane, enter **V_VCHCODE** for
the parameter name. Right-click the Parameters node and create
seven more parameters, as shown in Figure 17-10.

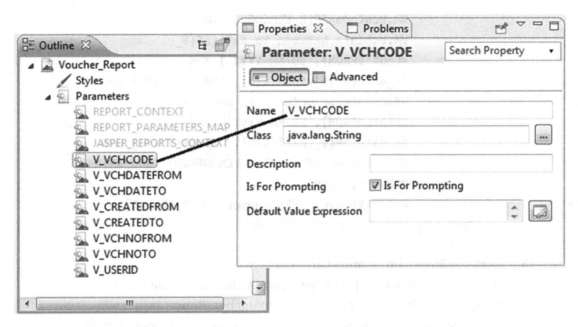

Figure 17-10. *Adding Report Parameters*

12. Click the **DataSet and Query editor dialog** icon (see Figure 17-6).
Add the following bold-faced clauses to the existing WHERE
clause:

Select CO.coname, VM.Vchcode,VCH.Vchtitle,VM.Vchno,VM.
Vchdate,VM.Vchdescription,
VM.createdby,VM.createdon, VD.line_no,VD.
COAcode,COA.COAtitle,VD.CCCode,CC.CCTitle,
VD.Vchdr,VD.Vchcr,VD.Vchreference,
(SELECT TO_CHAR(SYSDATE, 'DD-MON-YYYY HH24:MI:SS')
FROM DUAL) NOW

  From GL_COMPANY CO, GL_VOUCHER VCH, GL_COA COA, GL_COST_
CENTER CC, GL_TRAN_MASTER VM, GL_TRAN_DETAIL VD

Where VM.cocode=CO.cocode AND VM.tran_no=VD.tran_no AND
VM.Vchcode=VCH.Vchcode AND
VD.cocode=COA.cocode AND VD.COAcode=COA.COAcode AND
VD.CCCode=CC.CCCode(+) **AND**

```
          VM.VchCode=$P{V_VCHCODE}   AND
          VM.Vchdate between to_date($P{V_
          VCHDATEFROM},'DD-MM-YYYY') and
          to_date($P{V_VCHDATETO}, 'DD-MM-YYYY') AND
          VM.Createdon between to_date($P{V_
          CREATEDFROM},'DD-MM-YYYY') and
          to_date($P{V_CREATEDTO}, 'DD-MM-YYYY') AND
          VM.vchno BETWEEN  $P{V_VCHNOFROM}  and $P{V_
          VCHNOTO}  AND
          upper(VM.createdby)=upper( $P{V_USERID})
   Order By VCHCODE,VCHNO,LINE_NO
```

13.   Click the **Save** icon or press Ctrl+S to save your report. In the
      Design view, click **Compile Report**, as illustrated in Figure 17-11. A
      compiled version of the report named Voucher_Report.jasper will
      be created in the folder where the actual report file Voucher_Report.
      jrxml is saved. The report is ready, so close Jasper Studio.

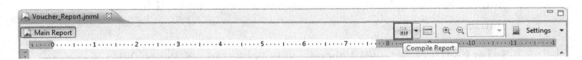

Figure 17-11. *Compiling Report in JasperStudio*

17.7 Copy the Compiled Report

After creating and compiling your report in Jasper Studio, your next move is to copy the
compiled version of your report (Voucher_Report.jasper) to C:\Program Files\Apache
Software Foundation\Tomcat 8.5\webapps\JasperReportsIntegration\WEB-INF\reports
folder.

17.8 Integrating Report with Oracle APEX

In these final set of steps, you will learn how to integrate your report with Oracle
APEX. Execute the instructions provided in the following sections in Oracle APEX.

17.8.1 Create a List of Values

Using Table 17-1, create a dynamic LOV from scratch. It contains a list of users and will be used in the next section to print only those vouchers that were recorded by the user selected from the list.

Table 17-1. *Dynamic LOV Attributes*

Action	Attribute	Value
Create LOV	Name	Users
	Type	Dynamic
	Query	SELECT userid d, userid r FROM gl_users
		WHERE cocode=(select cocode from gl_users where
		userid = :APP_USER)

17.8.2 Create the Parameters Form

Create a blank page and follow the instructions in Table 17-2 to add parameter components.

Table 17-2. *Parameters Form Attributes*

Action	Attribute	Value
Create Blank Page	Page Number	71
	Name	Vouchers Report
	Page Mode	Normal
	Breadcrumb	—Do not use breadcrumbs on page—
	Navigation Preference	Identify an existing navigation menu entry for this page.
	Existing Navigation Menu Entry	Reports

(continued)

Table 17-2. (*continued*)

Action	Attribute	Value
Create Region	Title	Vouchers Report
	Type	Static Content
	Template	Standard
Create Page Item	Name	P71_VCHCODE
	Type	Select List
	Label	Voucher Type
	Region	Vouchers Report
	Template	Required
	Label Column Span	2
	Value Required	Yes
	LOV Type	Shared Component
	Shared Component	Voucher Types
	Display Null Value	No
Create Page Item	Name	P71_VCHDATEFROM
	Type	Date Picker
	Label	Voucher Date
	Region	Vouchers Report
	Template	Required
	Label Column Span	2
	Format Mask	DD-MON-YYYY
	Value Required	Yes

(*continued*)

Table 17-2. (*continued*)

Action	Attribute	Value
Create Page Item	Name	P71_VCHDATETO
	Type	Date Picker
	Label	*Clear Label Box*
	Region	Vouchers Report
	Template	Required
	Label Column Span	2
	Format Mask	DD-MON-YYYY
	Value Required	Yes
Create Page Item	Name	P71_CREATEDFROM
	Type	Date Picker
	Label	Creation Date
	Region	Vouchers Report
	Template	Required
	Label Column Span	2
	Format Mask	DD-MON-YYYY
	Value Required	Yes
	Default Type	PL/SQL Expression
	PL/SQL Expression	SYSDATE

(*continued*)

Table 17-2. (*continued*)

Action	Attribute	Value
Create Page Item	Name	P71_CREATEDTO
	Type	Date Picker
	Label	*Clear Label Box*
	Region	Vouchers Report
	Template	Required
	Label Column Span	2
	Format Mask	DD-MON-YYYY
	Default Type	PL/SQL Expression
	PL/SQL Expression	SYSDATE
Create Page Item	Name	P71_VCHNOFROM
	Type	Text Field
	Label	Voucher Number
	Region	Vouchers Report
	Template	Required
	Label Column Span	2
	Value Required	Yes
	Default Type	Static Value
	Static Value	1 *(from minimum voucher number)*
Create Page Item	Name	P71_VCHNOTO
	Type	Text Field
	Label	*Clear Label Box*
	Region	Vouchers Report
	Template	Required
	Label Column Span	2
	Value Required	Yes

(*continued*)

Table 17-2. (*continued*)

Action	Attribute	Value
	Default Type	Static Value
	Static Value	9999999999 *(to maximum voucher number)*
Create Page Item	Name	P71_USERID
	Type	Select List
	Label	Created By
	Region	Vouchers Report
	Template	Required
	Label Column Span	2
	Value Required	Yes
	LOV Type	Shared Component
	List of Values	Users
	Display Null Value	No
	Default Type	PL/SQL Expression
	PL/SQL Expression	V('APP_USER') *(show id of the logged in user)*
Create Button	Button Name	Print
	Label	Print
	Region	Vouchers Report
	Button Position	Copy
	Hot	Yes
	Action	Submit Page

Click the Processing tab, right-click the Processing node, and select **Create Process**. Set the following attributes for this new process, which is being added to connect to your Jasper Report Sever and pass report parameters.

Property	Value
Name	Print Vouchers Report
Type	PL/SQL Code
PL/SQL CODE	

```
declare
  l_additional_parameters varchar2(32767);
begin
  xlib_jasperreports.set_report_url('http://localhost:8888/JasperReportsIntegration/report');

-- construct additional parameter list
  l_additional_parameters := 'V_VCHCODE=' || apex_util.url_encode(:P71_VCHCODE);
  l_additional_parameters := l_additional_parameters || '&V_VCHDATEFROM=' || apex_util.url_encode(:P71_VCHDATEFROM);
  l_additional_parameters := l_additional_parameters || '&V_VCHDATETO=' || apex_util.url_encode(:P71_VCHDATETO);
  l_additional_parameters := l_additional_parameters || '&V_CREATEDFROM=' || apex_util.url_encode(:P71_CREATEDFROM);
  l_additional_parameters := l_additional_parameters || '&V_CREATEDTO=' || apex_util.url_encode(:P71_CREATEDTO);
  l_additional_parameters := l_additional_parameters || '&V_VCHNOFROM=' || apex_util.url_encode(:P71_VCHNOFROM);
  l_additional_parameters := l_additional_parameters || '&V_VCHNOTO=' || apex_util.url_encode(:P71_VCHNOTO);
  l_additional_parameters := l_additional_parameters || '&V_USERID=' || apex_util.url_encode(:P71_USERID);

  xlib_jasperreports.show_report (p_rep_name => 'Voucher_Report',
                  p_rep_format => 'pdf',
                  p_data_source => 'default',
                  p_rep_locale => 'en-US',
                  p_out_filename => 'Voucher_Report.PDF',
                  p_additional_params => l_additional_parameters);
-- stop rendering of the current APEX page
  apex_application.g_unrecoverable_error := true;
end;
```

Point	Processing
When Button Pressed	PRINT

Run the page, provide report parameters and click the **Print** button. You will encounter an error: "*SyntaxError: Unexpected token % in JSON at position 0*". Switch back to the design area and click the root node: Page 71: Vouchers Report. In the properties pane, scroll down to the *Advanced* section and set *Reload on Submit* to **Always**. Click **Save** and reload the page. Click **Print**. This time the report will be downloaded to your PC as a PDF.

17.9 Summary

Printing reports in Oracle APEX was a real challenge in the past, but now things have changed. As you just experienced, you can design any type of report in JasperStudio and can quickly integrate it with your APEX application. In the next chapter, you will go through another important accounting report called Ledger.

CHAPTER 18

Ledger Report

A ledger report is a report that shows all financial activities performed in an account. In this application, it consists of seven columns, as illustrated later in the chapter in Figure 18-1. When a voucher is saved, all transactions you define in it are posted to the relevant ledger accounts with the respective debit and credit figures. The ledger report shows accounts with their transactions and balances. To generate this report, you use the Ledger Report Parameters form, where you specify the duration and the range of accounts you want to browse. As you can see, the parameter form has two buttons: the Display button is used to produce an onscreen view of the ledger report, while the Print button produces a hard copy. A useful ability of the report is that it contains a link for viewing the source voucher. This link will be created on the Voucher Date column.

18.1 Create Page and Parameters Form

The Ledger report segment will be created using a blank page containing two regions, as listed in Table 18-1. The first region will receive report parameters, and the second (to be created in the next section) will show the ledger report onscreen. You will add two pop-up LOVs to the parameter form. Using these LOVs, users will select financial accounts from the COA. Note that the COA Entry Level LOV will show only transaction-level accounts (i.e., level 4 accounts).

© Riaz Ahmed 2019
R. Ahmed, *Cloud Computing Using Oracle Application Express*,
https://doi.org/10.1007/978-1-4842-4243-8_18

Table 18-1. *Page and Parameters Form Attributes*

Action	Attribute	Value
Create Blank Page	Page Number	72
	Name	Ledger Report
	Page Mode	Normal
	Breadcrumb	—Do not use breadcrumbs on page—
	Navigation Preference	Identify an existing navigation menu entry for this page.
	Existing Navigation Menu Entry	Reports
Create Region	Title	Ledger Report Parameters
	Type	Static Content
	Template	Standard
Create Page Item	Name	P72_FROM
	Type	Date Picker
	Label	From
	Region	Ledger Report Parameters
	Label Column Span	2
	Template	Required
	Value Required	Yes
	Source Type	SQL Query (return single value) *(select fiscal year's starting date)*

(continued)

Table 18-1. (*continued*)

Action	Attribute	Value

	SQL Query	SELECT pfrom From gl_fiscal_year
		WHERE cocode=(select cocode from gl_users
		        where userid = :APP_USER)
		        AND
		     coyear=(select coyear from gl_users
		        where userid = :APP_USER)
		        AND
		comonthid=1

	Source Used	Only when current value in session state is null
Create Page Item	Name	P72_TO
	Label	To
	Region	Ledger Report Parameters
	Label Column Span	2
	Template	Required
	Value Required	Yes
	Source Type	SQL Query (return single value) *(select fiscal year's closing date)*

	SQL Query	SELECT pto FROM gl_fiscal_year
		WHERE cocode=(select cocode from gl_users
		        where userid = :APP_USER)
		        AND
		     coyear=(select coyear from gl_users
		        where userid = :APP_USER)
		        AND
		comonthid=12

	Source Used	Only when current value in session state is null

(*continued*)

Table 18-1. (*continued*)

Action	Attribute	Value
Create Page Item	Name	P72_ACCOUNTFROM
	Type	Popup LOV
	Label	\From Account\
	Region	Ledger Report Parameters
	Label Column Span	2
	Template	Required
	Value Required	Yes
	LOV Type	Shared Component
	List of Values	COA Entry Level
Create Page Item	Name	P72_ACCOUNTTO
	Type	Popup LOV
	Label	\To Account\
	Region	Ledger Report Parameters
	Label Column Span	2
	Template	Required
	LOV Type	Shared Component
	List of Values	COA Entry Level
Create Button	Button Name	Display
	Label	Display
	Region	Ledger Report Parameters
	Button Position	Copy
	Action	Submit Page

(*continued*)

Table 18-1. (*continued*)

Action	Attribute	Value
Create Button	Button Name	Print
	Label	Print
	Region	Ledger Report Parameters
	Button Position	Copy
	Action	Submit Page

18.2 Create an Interactive Report Region

Using Table 18-2, create an interactive report region to produce the onscreen version of the ledger report. The SELECT statement used in this report comprises two subqueries joined together using a UNION ALL set operator. The first subquery calculates opening balances of accounts by summing up all debit and credit figures recorded before the From date, specified in the P72_FROM date picker item. The second subquery fetches all transactions recorded between the two selected dates, inclusive. These are the transactions that you want to see in the ledger report. The queries also contain filters to process only those accounts selected in the two pop-up lists.

Table 18-2. *Interactive Report Region*

Action	Attribute	Value
Create Region	Title	Ledger
	Type	Interactive Report
	Type (under Source)	SQL Query
	SQL Query	Book_Code\Chapter18\IR SQL Query 18.2.txt
	Template	Standard

18.3 Formatting Ledger Report

Execute the following steps to format the Ledger Interactive Report:

1. Set the Type attribute to Hidden Column for both the VCHCODE and TRAN_NO columns.

2. Modify the VCHDR, VCHCR, and BALANCE columns by applying a format mask ($5,234.10) to all three of them.

3. Add appropriate headings to all columns, as shown in Figure 18-1.

4. Run this segment from the Ledgers menu under the Reports menu. Select the date you entered for the first voucher you created in Chapter 14 in both date boxes, or specify a long range to fetch that transaction. Also select account of A.B. Enterprises (the account you selected in that voucher) in both pop-up LOVs, and hit the Display button.

5. Click the Actions menu. Select Data followed by the Sort option. Select the columns in this order: COACODE (Code), VCHDATE (Voucher Date), and VCHNO (Voucher Number). Keep Direction as Ascending and Null Sorting as Default. This step will sort the interactive report first on account codes, then on voucher dates, and finally on voucher numbers. The new column names, appearing within parentheses, were provided in Step 3. Click the Apply button to save your changes.

6. Click the Actions menu again. Select Format and then Control Break. Select COACODE (Code) in the first row and COATITLE (Title) in the second row. Click Apply. This action will place a control break to display each account separately.

7. Click the Actions menu. Select Format and then Highlight. Set the highlight rule Name to Opening Balance, Highlight Type to Row, Background Color to Blue, Text Color to White, Condition Column to Description, Operator to Like, and Expression to Opening Balance%. Click Apply. This rule is created to highlight opening balances of accounts using different colors.

8. Click the Actions menu. Select Data and then Aggregate. Set Aggregation to New Aggregation, Function to Sum, Column to VCHDR (which should be Debit after renaming). Click Apply. This will add a grand total figure for each account after summing up all the values in the debit column.

9. Repeat Step 8 for the VCHCR (Credit) column.

10. Click Actions and select Save Report. Select the Save option As Default Report Settings, set Default Report Type to Primary, and click Apply to save these modifications.

11. In the second LOV, select the ABN AMRO bank account that you used in Chapter 14, and hit the Display button to refresh the report, which should now display the two ledgers with the grand totals and individual current balances of these accounts, as shown in Figure 18-1.

18.4 Get Ledger Report in PDF

Since the process of creating the ledger PDF is similar to the vouchers report process that you saw in the previous chapter, I won't repeat it here. I've provided the corresponding report query in the Book Code Chapter18 folder.

18.5 Drill Down to Source Voucher

While scrutinizing a ledger, an accountant may want to see the complete details of a specific transaction appearing in that ledger. To facilitate the accountant, you will provide a link for each transaction in the ledger interactive report to allow easy navigation to the source voucher. Execute the instructions provided in the following sections to add this functionality.

18.5.1 Create Link in Interactive Report

Expand the Columns node in the Ledger Interactive Report region and set the attributes listed in Table 18-3 for the VCHDATE column. This is the column that will act as a link between the ledger and source voucher. The link is created on the date column, and it calls page 44 (created next) to display details of the clicked transaction. It also forwards three values to items on page 44 from the Voucher Master section.

Table 18-3. *Link in Interactive Report*

Action	Attribute	Value	
Modify Report Column	Column Name	VCHDATE	
	Type	Link	
	Target	Type = Page In This Application	
		Page = 44	
		Set Items	
		Name	**Value**
		P44_VCHDATE	#VCHDATE#
		P44_VCHCODE	#VCHCODE#
		P44_VCHNO	#VCHNO#
		Clear Cache = 44	
	Link Text	#VCHDATE#	

18.5.2 Create Voucher Page

Execute the following steps to create a new page to display the selected voucher when a link is clicked in the Ledger Report:

1. Create a new page (page 44) from page 43 using the Copy utility as described previously for the Voucher Verification segment. Name the new page **Drilled Down Voucher** and associate it with the Reports menu.

2. Modify the Transaction Details region on page 44 by replacing the existing SQL query with Book_Code\Chapter18\Drilled Down Voucher.txt.

3. In the previous section, you passed three page items from the Ledger Interactive Report to this page. However, there is a fourth one (Description) that is displayed in the voucher's master section. Since the master description was not fetched in the interactive report query, you will adopt another technique to fetch a value for this item using the three key values defined on the previous page. On page 44, click the P44_VCHDESCRIPTION item and then set the attributes listed in Table 18-4.

Table 18-4. *P44_VCHDESCRIPTION Attributes*

Attribute	Value
Source Type	SQL Query (return single value)

SQL Query	SELECT vchdescription
	FROM gl_tran_master
	WHERE vchdate=:P44_VCHDATE AND
	      vchcode=:P44_VCHCODE AND
	      vchno=:P44_VCHNO

Source Used	Always, replacing any existing value in session state

4. Click the Cancel button. Set its label to **Back to Ledger** and replace the existing Page attribute value (under Target) from 42 to **72** to move back to the ledger report page.

5. Delete all other buttons, all validations, and all processes.

18.6 Test Your Work

That's it—you're done! The ledger report is ready for a test drive. Invoke it from the Reports menu and pass different parameters (as illustrated in Figure 18-1) to check both the onscreen and PDF versions. You can optionally add a print button to page 44 that will allow users to print the selected voucher without leaving the interface. You can find its report query in the `Print Drilled Down Voucher.txt` file.

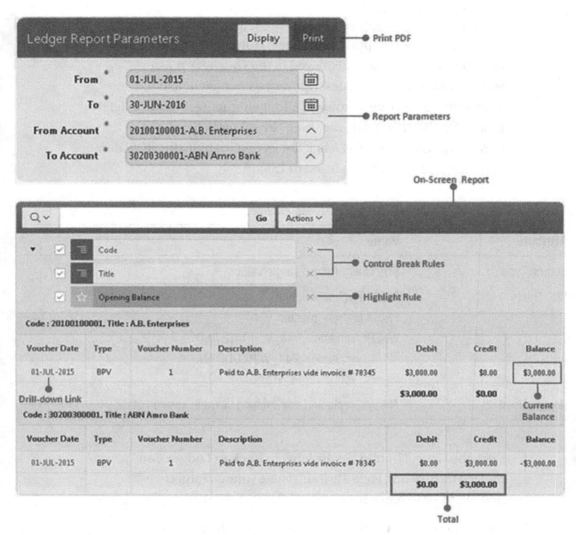

Figure 18-1. *Ledger report*

18.7 Summary

Using a ledger report, you can view the activities and balances of accounts with a few clicks. If you want to see a summarized report of all accounts, move on to the next chapter to create a trial balance report.

CHAPTER 19

Trial Balance Report

The trial balance report shows the summarized balances of accounts up to a specific date. It delivers the opening balance, activity, and closing balance of each account. Unlike the Ledger Report, this report can be produced for any level. For example, you can run a Trial Balance Report for the first level only simply to see top-level account activities. You can also filter the report to display a specific range of financial accounts from the COA along with a cost center, should you want to see account balances for only one cost center. The parameters form has just one date picker from where you select the date up to which closing balances are calculated and displayed in the report.

19.1 Trial Balance Report Table

The transaction data, entered through vouchers, are stored in the gl_tran_master and gl_tran_detail tables. After generating the trial balance report from these two tables, you store the result in the following temporary table. It holds trial balance data for each user until the user runs the report again. The data in this table is populated through a process to be created later in Table 19-4.

```
CREATE TABLE gl_trial_balance
(coacode VARCHAR2(11), coatitle VARCHAR2(50), coalevel NUMBER(1), opendr
NUMBER(15,2), opencr NUMBER(15,2), activitydr NUMBER(15,2), activitycr
NUMBER(15,2), closingdr NUMBER(15,2), closingcr NUMBER(15,2),
coname VARCHAR2(50), tbdate DATE, fromaccount VARCHAR2(11), toaccount
VARCHAR2(11), cccode VARCHAR2(5),
cctitle VARCHAR2(25), reportlevel NUMBER(1), userid VARCHAR2(50),
grand_total NUMBER(1))
```

© Riaz Ahmed 2019
R. Ahmed, *Cloud Computing Using Oracle Application Express*,
https://doi.org/10.1007/978-1-4842-4243-8_19

19.2 Create a List of Values

Using Table 19-1, create a LOV from scratch. It will be used to allow you to select any account level for the trial balance report. If you run this report for the transaction level (level 4), all parent levels (i.e., 1, 2, and 3) also appear on the report by default, unless you put a check on the parameter option labeled Print Selected Level.

Table 19-1. *LOV Attributes*

Action	Attribute	Value
Create LOV	Name	COA All Levels
	Type	Dynamic
	Query	SELECT coacode||'-'||coatitle d, coacode r FROM gl_coa WHERE cocode=(select cocode from gl_users where userid = :APP_USER) ORDER BY coacode

19.3 Create Page and Parameters Form

Using Table 19-2, create a blank page and its components for this segment.

Table 19-2. *Page and Component Attributes*

Action	Attribute	Value
Create Blank Page	Page Number	73
	Name	Trial Balance Report
	Page Mode	Normal
	Breadcrumb	—Don't use breadcrumbs on page—
	Navigation Preference	Identify an existing navigation menu entry for this page.
	Existing Navigation Menu Entry	Reports

(*continued*)

Table 19-2. (*continued*)

Action	Attribute	Value
Create Region	Title	Trial Balance Report Parameters
	Type	Static Content
	Template	Standard
Create Page Item	Name	P73_ACCOUNTFROM
	Type	Popup LOV
	Label	From Account
	Region	Trial Balance Report Parameters
	Label Column Span	2
	Template	Required
	Value Required	Yes
	LOV Type	Shared Component
	List of Values	COA All Levels
Create Page Item	Name	P73_ACCOUNTTO
	Type	Popup LOV
	Label	To Account
	Region	Trial Balance Report Parameters
	Label Column Span	2
	Template	Required
	Value Required	Yes
	LOV Type	Shared Component
	List of Values	COA All Levels
Create Page Item	Name	P73_CCCODE
	Type	Pop-up LOV
	Label	Cost Center
	Region	Trial Balance Report Parameters

(*continued*)

Table 19-2. (*continued*)

Action	Attribute	Value
	Label Column Span	2
	Template	Optional
	Value Required	No
	LOV Type	Shared Component
	List of Values	Cost Centers
Create Page Item	Name	P73_COALEVEL
	Type	Text Field
	Label	Account Level
	Region	Trial Balance Report Parameters
	Label Column Span	2
	Template	Required
	Value Required	Yes
	Default Type	Static Value
	Static Value	4 *(display report for all levels)*
Create Page Item	Name	P73_TBDATE
	Type	Date Picker
	Label	As On
	Region	Trial Balance Report Parameters
	Label Column Span	2
	Template	Required
	Value Required	Yes
	Default Type	PL/SQL Expression
	PL/SQL Expression	SYSDATE
Create Button	Button Name	Display
	Label	Display
	Region	Trial Balance Report Parameters

(*continued*)

Table 19-2. (*continued*)

Action	Attribute	Value
	Button Position	Copy
	Action	Submit Page
Create Button	Button Name	Print
	Label	Print
	Region	Trial Balance Report Parameters
	Button Position	Copy
	Action	Submit Page

19.4 Create the Interactive Report Region

Using Table 19-3, add an Interactive Report region to the page. It will produce an onscreen version of the Trial Balance Report. It is based on a SELECT statement that fetches the report of the current user from the GL_TRIAL_BALANCE table. The table is populated using a process defined in the next section.

Table 19-3. *Interactive Report Region Attributes*

Action	Attribute	Value
Create Region	Title	Trial Balance
	Type	Interactive Report
	Type (under Source)	SQL Query
	SQL Query	SELECT * FROM gl_trial_balance
		WHERE userid = :APP_USER
		ORDER BY coacode

19.5 Create a Process to Generate Trial Balance

The process mentioned in Table 19-4 uses a cursor based on the COA of the logged-in user. The cursor loops through every COA record to calculate account balances. These balances, along with other relevant information, are inserted into the GL_TRIAL_BALANCE table with the user ID. After completing the loop, a record is added to the end of the table that shows the grand total for each column. The process is executed when either the Display or Print button is clicked.

Table 19-4. *Process to Generate Trial Balance*

Action	Attribute	Value
Create Process	Name	Generate Trial Balance
	Type	PL/SQL Code
	PL/SQL Code	Book_Code\Chapter19\Generate Trial Balance.txt
	Point	Processing
	Server-side Condition	Request is contained in Value
	Value	Display,Print

19.6 Formatting the Trial Balance Report

Execute the following steps to format the Interactive Report:

1. Add the appropriate headings to columns as Code, Title, Opening Debit, Opening Credit, Activity Debit, Activity Credit, Closing Debit, and Closing Credit.

2. Modify all the numeric columns to apply the number format mask.

3. Run this module from the Trial Balance option in the Reports menu. Select the values shown in Figure 19-1 in the Parameters region and hit the Display button. At this stage, the report will show the balances of just two accounts along with their group accounts. These are the same accounts you entered in the first voucher.

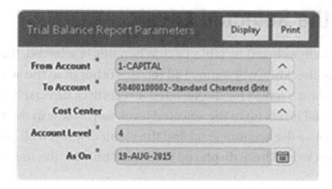

Figure 19-1. *Report parameters*

4.   Click the Actions menu and then click the Select Columns
     option. Move the CCCODE, CCTITLE, COALEVEL, CONAME,
     FROMACCOUNT, REPORTLEVEL, TBDATE, TOACCOUNT,
     USERID, and GRAND TOTAL columns to the Do Not Display
     pane, leaving the Code, Title, Opening Debit, Opening Credit,
     Activity Debit, Activity Credit, Closing Debit, and Closing Credit
     columns in the Display in Report section. Click Apply.

5.   Click the Actions menu again. Select Data ➤ Sort. Select CODE in
     the first row, keep Direction as Ascending, and keep Null Sorting
     as Default to sort the report on the Code column. Click Apply.

6.   Add a highlight rule (as mentioned in the Formatting Ledger
     Report section in Chapter 18) for the Grand Total row, using Title
     and GRAND_TOTAL% as Column and Expression, respectively.
     Click Apply.

7.   Click Actions ➤ Format ➤ Rows per Page and select the All option
     to show all records.

8.   Click Actions and select Save Report. Select the option As Default
     Report Settings, set Default Report Type to Primary, and click
     Apply to save the report.

19.7 Print the Selected Level

Create a checkbox item as listed in Table 19-5. When this is selected, the process associated with this checkbox will remove all records other than the selected level to display a Trial Balance report for the selected level only. Conversely, keeping it unchecked displays all levels up to the selected level, as you saw in the previous section where you selected 4 as the account level and the result displayed all parent levels. Checking this option would have displayed the report only for the transaction-level accounts.

Table 19-5. *Check Box Attributes*

Action	Attribute	Value
Create Page Item	Name	P73_SELECTEDLEVEL
	Type	Checkbox
	Label	*Clear Label*
	Number of Columns	1
	Region	Trial Balance Report Parameters
	Template	Optional
	Label Column Span	2
	LOV Type	Static Values
	Static Values	STATIC:Print Selected Level;Y

19.7.1 Create Process

The process listed in Table 19-6 is associated with the previous checkbox to display/print accounts for the selected level.

Table 19-6. *Process Attributes*

Action	Attribute	Value
Create Process	Name	Print Selected Level
	Type	PL/SQL Code
	PL/SQL Code	DELETE FROM gl_trial_balance WHERE coalevel <> :P73_COALEVEL AND userid = :APP_USER;
	Point	Processing
	Server-side Condition	Item = Value
	Item	P73_SELECTEDLEVEL
	Value	Y

19.8 Eliminate Zero Balances

As the name suggests, the process (created later in Table 19-8) associated with the checkbox created in Table 19-7 will eliminate all records that have no balances at all. This feature will make the report smaller because it removes those records from the Trial Balance Report with zero balances.

Table 19-7. *Checkbox Attributes*

Action	Attribute	Value
Create Page Item	Name	P73_ZEROBALANCE
	Type	Checkbox
	Label	*Clear Label*
	Number of Columns	1
	Region	Trial Balance Report Parameters
	Template	Optional

(continued)

Table 19-7. (*continued*)

Action	Attribute	Value
	Label Column Span	2
	LOV Type	Static Values
	Static Values	STATIC:Eliminate Zero Balances;Y
	Default Type	Static Value
	Static Value	Y *(all zero balance records will be eliminated by default)*

19.8.1 Create a Process

Create the process shown in Table 19-8. The process will eliminate accounts with zero balance.

Table 19-8. *Process Attributes*

Action	Attribute	Value
Create Process	Name	Eliminate Zero Balances
	Type	PL/SQL Code
	PL/SQL Code	DELETE FROM gl_trial_balance WHERE nvl(opendr,0) = 0 AND nvl(opencr,0) = 0 AND nvl(activitydr,0) = 0 AND nvl(activitycr,0) = 0 AND nvl(closingdr,0) = 0 AND nvl(closingcr,0) = 0 AND userid=:APP_USER;
	Point	Processing
	Server-side Condition	Item = Value
	Item	P73_ZEROBALANCE
	Value	Y

19.9 Create a Validation

The validation listed in Table 19-9 will check the data for the existence of report criteria.

Table 19-9. *Validation Attributes*

Action	Attribute	Value
Create Validation	Name	Check Data
	Type	PL/SQL Function (returning Error Text)
	PL/SQL Function	Book_Code\Chapter19\Check Data.txt
	Server-side Condition	Request is contained in Value
	Value	Display,Print

19.10 Get the Trial Balance Report in PDF

Create a PDF version of the Trial Balance Report using the instructions provided earlier in Chapter 17.

19.11 Drill Down to the Ledger Report

Just like the link that you created in the Ledger Report to access the source voucher, you will create a link here on the Code column to access the Ledger Report from within the trial balance. Expand the Trial Balance Report's Columns node and set the attributes in Table 19-10 for the COACODE column. Recall that you needed two account codes and two date parameters to call the Ledger Report. The values declared in the attributes in Table 19-10 forward account code information to the Ledger page. The dates are calculated by the Target page itself using a couple of SELECT statements.

Table 19-10. *Code Column Link Attributes*

Action	Attribute	Value	
Modify Report Column	Column Name	COACODE	
	Type	Link	
	Target	Type = Page In This Application	
		Page = 72	
		Set Items	
		Name	**Value**
		P72_ACCOUNTFROM	#COACODE#
		P72_ACCOUNTTO	#COACODE#
		Clear Cache = 72	
	Link Text	#COACODE#	

19.12 Test Your Work

Run the Trial Balance Report first by passing a complete COA range, as shown in Figure 19-2. Also, try the report by selecting specific accounts and enabling/disabling the optional parameters provided on the page. Note that although the drill-down function applies to all levels (in other words, all account codes appear as links irrespective of levels), the Ledger Report will display data for the transaction level only.

Figure 19-2. *Trial Balance Report*

19.13 Summary

The Trial Balance Report here not only displays summarized balances of accounts, but the online view of this report helps you drill down to an account ledger and then from the ledger account to the source transaction. The next few chapters deal with bank transactions.

CHAPTER 20

Opening Bank Transactions

The application provides you with a complete module to deal with your banking. Recall that while creating accounts in the chart of accounts (COA) you used a specific type to mark bank accounts; that was the first step in the bank reconciliation process. In addition, the application allows you to reconcile the bank transactions recorded through vouchers with the statements provided by your banks. But, before that, you have to incorporate some bank transactions into this application. These are the transactions recorded either manually or in another system and were not reconciled with the banks. In this chapter, you'll record all such transactions into a separate table that will keep appearing on the Bank Reconciliation page and report unless you mark them as reconciled. The actual reconciliation process will be created in Chapter 21.

TABLE TO RECORD OPENING BANK TRANSACTIONS

```
CREATE TABLE gl_banks_os
(sr_no NUMBER, Cocode NUMBER CONSTRAINT fk_banks_os1 REFERENCES GL_Company
(Cocode) NOT NULL,
coacode VARCHAR2(11) NOT NULL, remarks VARCHAR2(50) NOT NULL, vchdr
NUMBER(15,2) NOT NULL,
vchcr NUMBER(15,2) NOT NULL, reconciled NUMBER(1) NOT NULL, CONSTRAINT
pk_banks_os PRIMARY KEY (sr_no), CONSTRAINT fk_banks_os2 FOREIGN KEY
(cocode,coacode) REFERENCES GL_COA)

CREATE SEQUENCE gl_banks_os_seq MINVALUE 1 START WITH 1 INCREMENT BY 1 CACHE 20
```

© Riaz Ahmed 2019
R. Ahmed, *Cloud Computing Using Oracle Application Express*,
https://doi.org/10.1007/978-1-4842-4243-8_20

20.1 Create Page

Using Table 20-1, create a new Form page. Select Editable Interactive Grid on the second wizard screen. Set the rest of the attributes for the page as follows.

Table 20-1. *Page Attributes*

Wizard Screen	Attribute	Value
Page Attributes	Page Number	17
	Page Name	Opening Banks Outstanding
	Page Mode	Normal
Navigation Menu	Navigation Preference	Identify an existing navigation menu entry for this page.
	Existing Navigation Menu Entry	Setup
Report Source	Source Type	Table
	Table/View Name	GL_BANKS_OS
	Primary Key Column	SR_NO
	Columns	Select All Columns from the table

20.2 Modify Region Source Query

Edit the Opening Banks Outstanding region and modify the Region Source query by adding the WHERE clause in Table 20-2. This clause is added to fetch the records of the company to which the user belongs. The clause retrieves only those entries that are still unreconciled.

Table 20-2. *Opening Banks Outstanding Region Attributes*

Action	Attribute	Value
Modify Region	SQL Query	SELECT "SR_NO", "COCODE", "REMARKS", "COACODE", "VCHDR", "VCHCR", "RECONCILED" FROM "#OWNER#"."GL_BANKS_OS" **WHERE cocode=(select cocode from gl_users where userid=:APP_USER) AND reconciled=0**

Expand the Columns node under the Opening Banks Outstanding region and perform the following modifications:

1. Set the Type attribute of the SR_NO, COCODE, and RECONCILED columns to Hidden to hide these columns.

2. Type appropriate headings for the four visible columns:

   Bank Code, **Remarks**, **Debit**, and **Credit**.

3. Edit the COACODE column. Set its Type to Popup LOV, set List of Values Type to SQL Query, and enter the following SQL statement in the SQL Query box to display the bank accounts of the current company in the popup LOV. Set the Width attribute of this column to **50**.

```
SELECT coacode||'-'||coatitle d, coacode r FROM
gl_coa
WHERE cocode=(select cocode from gl_users where
userid=:APP_USER) AND coatype='Bank'
ORDER BY coacode
```

4. Modify the VCHDR, VCHCR, and RECONCILED columns and set their Default Type values to PL/SQL Expression and setPL/ SQL Expression to **0**. This way the three columns will have zero as the default value.

5. Set the Width attribute of the Remarks column to **50**.

20.3 Modify Interactive Grid Column

Expand the Opening Banks Outstanding Interactive Grid region and set the following attributes as mentioned in Table 20-3 for the COCODE column:

Table 20-3. *Set Default Value for Company Code (COCODE) Column*

Action	Attribute	Value
Modify Column	Column Name	COCODE
	Default Type	SQL Query
	SQL Query	SELECT cocode from gl_users where userid=:APP_USER

20.4 Test Your Work

Run this segment from the Setup ➤ Opening Bank Transactions menu and execute the following steps:

1. From the Bank Code popup LOV, which should be displaying only bank accounts, select an account (e.g., ABN AMRO). Note that you can enter as many unsettled transactions as you need for a bank using this interface. For example, there are certain deposits not appearing in the bank statement. Similarly, the checks you issued to some creditors were not presented as well. You need to input all such cases on a separate row so that when you run the reconciliation segment, they appear individually as separate entries.

2. Enter something in the remarks column, such as **Opening outstanding as of 30th June 2015**.

3. Enter a numeric value (e.g., **10000**) in the Debit column and hit the Apply Changes button to save this entry. Figure 20-1 demonstrates some opening outstanding transactions.

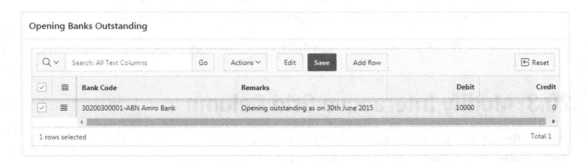

Figure 20-1. *Opening outstanding transactions*

20.5 Summary

This segment is helpful in the bank reconciliation process. After you record the outstanding transactions through this interface, you are ready to perform the reconciliation activity, as discussed in the next chapter.

CHAPTER 21

Bank Reconciliation

A bank reconciliation is the process by which you match your bank ledger transactions with those in your bank statement and attempt to find any differences between the two. All income transactions appearing on the debit side of your ledger are shown on the credit side of the bank statement. Conversely, all payments that you make are recorded on the credit side of your ledger, and the same transactions are reported on the debit side of the bank statement. This part of the application allows you to identify transactions and perform a reconciliation.

21.1 Create Page and Parameters Form

Using Table 21-1, create a blank page and add components to it. The page contains three regions. The first region (Parameters), which you are already familiar with, carries two radio buttons (Reconciled and Unreconciled) and a Select List showing all accounts marked as the Bank type from the chart of accounts (COA). The reconciled option displays all the records that you reconciled previously with the bank; all unsettled transactions are displayed when you select the Unreconciled option. Whenever you switch banks or select a different criterion from the radio group, the page is submitted to refresh the data.

© Riaz Ahmed 2019
R. Ahmed, *Cloud Computing Using Oracle Application Express*,
https://doi.org/10.1007/978-1-4842-4243-8_21

Table 21-1. *Blank Page Attributes*

Action	Attribute	Value
Create Blank Page	Page Number	51
	Name	Bank Reconciliation
	Page Mode	Normal
	Breadcrumb	—Do not use breadcrumbs on page—
	Navigation Preference	Identify an existing navigation menu entry for this page.
	Existing Navigation Menu Entry	Utilities
Create Region	Title	Bank Reconciliation Parameters
	Type	Static Content
	Template	Standard
Create Page Item	Name	P51_CRITERIA
	Type	Radio Group
	Label	Show
	Number of Columns	2
	Page Action on Selection	Submit Page (*to show data according to the selected option*)
	Region	Bank Reconciliation Parameters
	Start New Row	Yes
	Column/Column Span	Automatic
	Template	Optional
	Label Column Span	2
	LOV Type	Static Values
	Static Values	STATIC:Reconciled;1,Unreconciled;0
	Display Null Value	No

(continued)

Table 21-1. *(continued)*

Action	Attribute	Value
	Default Type	Static Value
	Static Value	0
Create Page Item	Name	P51_BANKS
	Type	Select List
	Label	\Select a bank\
	Page Action on Selection	Submit Page (*to refresh report regions*)
	Region	Bank Reconciliation Parameters
	Start New Row	Yes
	Column/Column Span	Automatic
	Label Column Span	2
	Template	Required
	Value Required	Yes
	LOV Type	SQL Query
	SQL Query	SELECT coacode||'-' ||coatitle d, coacode r FROM gl_coa WHERE cocode= (select cocode from gl_users where userid=:APP_USER) AND coatype='Bank' ORDER BY coacode

21.2 Display Outstanding Opening Transactions

Create the following Interactive Report region to display all the outstanding bank transactions that you entered in Chapter 20. In the Application Builder interface, click the Create Page button and select the Form option followed by Report with Form on Table. Use the parameters given in Table 21-2 to complete the wizard. Note that when you provide a page number (on the Report Page screen) of a page that already exists, an Interactive Report is added to that page. Here, for example, an Interactive Report region will be added to page 51 along with a corresponding form on a separate page (page 52). All opening outstanding figures will be displayed on page 51 in an Interactive Report region. Using the edit link in this region, you can call the selected record on page 52 where it is displayed in a form to mark it either as reconciled or as unreconciled. Remember, the GL_BANKS_OS table has a flag column named Reconciled, which is attached to the radio items in the form on page 52. Also note that the form allows an update operation only on the Reconciled column.

Table 21-2. *Attributes of Report and Form Pages*

Wizard Screen	Attribute	Value
Page Attribute	Report Type	Interactive Report
	Report Page Number	51
	Report Page Name	Opening Outstanding
	Form Page Number	52
	Form Page Name	Reconcile Opening
	Form Page Mode	Modal Dialog
Navigation Menu	Existing Navigation Menu Entry	Utilities
Data Source	Table Name	GL_BANKS_OS
	Select Columns	Select all columns from the table.
Form Page	Primary Key Type	Select Primary Key Column(s)
	Select Columns	Select all columns
	Primary Key Column 1	SR_NO
	Source for PK Column	Existing Sequence
	Sequence	GL_BANKS_OS_SEQ

Modify the Report 1 Interactive Report region on page 51 as follows:

1. Set the title of this region to **Opening Outstanding**.

2. Add the following WHERE clause to the region's SQL Query:

```
WHERE cocode=(select cocode from gl_users where
userid=:APP_USER)
AND coacode=:P51_BANKS and reconciled=:P51_CRITERIA
```

3. Set Server-side Condition Type to Rows Returned and enter the
   following query in the SQL Query box. This condition will hide the
   report region when there is no record for the selected criterion.

```
SELECT 1 FROM "#OWNER#"."GL_BANKS_OS"
WHERE cocode=(select cocode from gl_users where
userid=:APP_USER) AND coacode=:P51_BANKS and
reconciled=:P51_CRITERIA
```

4. Hide the SR_NO, COCODE, COACODE, and RECONCILED
   columns by setting their Type attribute to Hidden Column.
   Change the headings for the VCHDR and VCHCR columns to
   Debit and Credit and set Include Search Bar (under Attributes
   node) to No to suppress the Interactive Report's search box.

21.3 Modify Reconcile Opening Form

Edit page 52 (the Reconcile Opening form) and modify the following items. You can
access this form from the Opening Outstanding Interactive Report on page 51 to mark an
opening outstanding transaction as reconciled. In the final step of this section, you will
transform the P52_RECONCILED item into a radio group with two options. Once you
mark an entry as reconciled and submit the change, it disappears from the unreconciled
list in the Interactive Report on page 51. Selecting the Reconciled radio option on page
51 reverses the entry.

1. Mark the P52_COCODE item as hidden.

2. Modify the labels of the page items coacode, vhcdr, and vchcr to
   Bank Code, Debit, and Credit, respectively.

3. Change the Type attribute of Bank Code, Remarks, Debit, and Credit items to Display Only. Set the Template property of these four page items to Optional.

4. Modify the P52_RECONCILED item using the attributes listed in Table 21-3.

Table 21-3. *P52_RECONCILED Attributes*

Attribute	Value
Type	Radio Group
Label	*Clear Label box*
Number of Columns	2
LOV Type	Static Values
Static Values	STATIC:Reconcile;1,Unreconcile;0
Display Null Values	No

21.4 Current Transactions Region

Edit page 51 to add another region. This region will have an Interactive Grid (IG) to display and reconcile current transactions entered through vouchers. It is based on a powerful SQL statement that fetches complete transaction information from three relevant tables based on the provided criteria and related to the current company. The statement also ensures that the fetched transactions are neither opening nor closing entries. Closing entries have nothing to do with the reconciliation process. Since you have already made exclusive provisions in the previous chapter for individual opening outstanding transactions of banks, opening balances are also exempt from this process. Opening balances are those values that you usually enter through a journal voucher when you switch to a new application from another system. For this application, you will create a voucher carrying the opening balances of accounts in Chapter 24. Note that the transaction table also includes a Reconciled flag column. A value of 1 in this column indicates that the corresponding transaction is reconciled. Create an Interactive Grid region using Table 21-4 to display current bank transactions.

Table 21-4. *Interactive Grid Region Attributes*

Action	Attribute	Value
Create Region	Title	Current Transactions
	Type	Interactive Grid
	SQL Query	SELECT "TD"."LINE_NO", "TM"."VCHDATE", "VCH"."VCHTYPE", "TM"."VCHNO", "TD"."VCHDESCRIPTION", nvl("TD"."VCHREFERENCE",'-') "VCHREFERENCE", "TD"."VCHDR", "TD"."VCHCR", "TD"."RECONCILED" FROM "GL_VOUCHER" "VCH", "GL_TRAN_MASTER" "TM", "GL_TRAN_DETAIL" "TD" WHERE "TM"."COCODE"="TD"."COCODE" AND "TM"."TRAN_NO"="TD"."TRAN_NO" AND "TM"."VCHCODE"="VCH"."VCHCODE" AND "TM"."CLOSING"=0 AND "TM"."VCHDESCRIPTION" <> 'OPENING BALANCES' AND "TM"."COCODE"=(select cocode from gl_users where userid=:APP_USER) AND "TD"."COACODE"=:P51_BANKS AND "TD"."RECONCILED"=:P51_CRITERIA

Modify the Interactive Grid region by executing the following steps. In Step 3, you change the Reconciled column to a radio group to display Yes and No. Initially you use this page item to reconcile transactions and later to reverse the reconciliation process.

1. Expand the Columns node. Click the LINE_NO column and set its Type to Hidden. Also, set Primary Key (under Source) to Yes.

2. For the VCHDR and VCHCR columns, set the heading and column alignments to the right.

3. Click the RECONCILED column and set the following attributes:

Attribute	Value
Type	Radio Group
Number of Columns	1
LOV Type	Static Values
Static Values	STATIC:Yes;1,No;0
Display Null Value	No

4. Enter meaningful column headings (Date, Type, Number, Description, Reference, Debit, Credit, and Reconcile).

5. Set the Query Only attribute (under Source) to Yes for VCHDATE, VCHTYPE, VCHNO, VCHDESCRIPTION, VCHREFERENCE, VCHDR, and VCHCR columns.

6. Click the Attributes node under the Current Transactions IG and set Enabled (under Edit) to Yes. In the Allowed Operations section, un-check Add Row and Delete Row options, leaving the Update option checked to make the IG editable.

21.5 Test Your Work

Right now you have just two entries to test this segment, one each in the opening outstanding and current transactions. Execute the following steps to perform a reconciliation using the Bank Reconciliation option from the Utilities menu. Figure 21-1 illustrates the three regions you created for this segment in this chapter.

1. Select the Unreconciled option in the parameters region followed by ABN Amro bank from the Banks list. The page gets refreshed and shows the two entries in their respective regions.

2. Start the reconciliation by clicking the edit link for the entry appearing in the Opening Outstanding region. This will open page 52 with the selected record. Select the Reconcile option from the radio group and click Apply Changes to mark the opening outstanding entry as reconciled. You are taken back to page 51, where the entry disappears.

3. On page 51, switch the Show option to Reconciled. The entry reappears in its region, but this time it is displayed as a reconciled entry. You can reverse it using the same edit link. Go ahead and test this functionality.

4. To reconcile current transactions, switch the Show option on page 51 back to the Unreconciled, select the Yes option in the Reconcile column for the sole entry appearing in the Current Transaction region, and click the Save button. Once again the entry will vanish from your screen and can be reinstated by selecting No in the Reconciled option, as you did in the previous step.

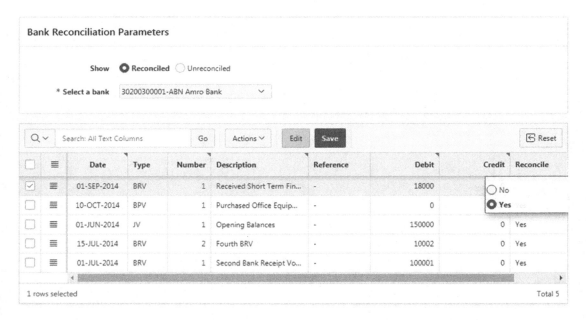

Figure 21-1. *Bank Reconciliation Page*

21.6 Summary

The bank reconciliation process helps you find discrepancies between your books of accounts and your bank statement. After completing this process, you call the Bank Reconciliation Report (created in the next chapter) that shows balances from both sides along with outstanding transactions (if any).

CHAPTER 22

Bank Reconciliation Report

Even after reconciling your ledger entries with those appearing in the bank statement, there might still be some unsettled transactions on both sides. For example, say a check was issued to a vendor that doesn't appear in the bank statement. Although it was recorded in the application, for some reason it was not presented to the bank in due course. Similarly, say the bank statement reports a credit amount deposited directly by one of your customers that you were not aware of. In the latter case, accountants prepare a receipt voucher to incorporate and reconcile the credit. For the former case, you have to wait until the check appears in a subsequent bank statement. After completing the reconciliation process, the application produces a report that shows the current ledger balance and a calculated bank statement balance, with some unsettled transactions (such as unpresented checks). The two balances should match, if there are no more outstanding figures on either side.

22.1 The Bank Reconciliation Report Table

In a similar way to the Trial Balance Report, the Bank Reconciliation Report is based on a table: gl_reconcile_report. Reconciliation reports are also stored for each user individually. The table also stores report parameters for display on the report.

```
CREATE TABLE gl_reconcile_report
(srno NUMBER, userid VARCHAR2(50), coname VARCHAR2(50), reportdate DATE,
coacode VARCHAR2(11),
coatitle VARCHAR2(50), monthyear VARCHAR2(14), vchdate DATE, vchtype
VARCHAR2(6), vchno NUMBER(10), vchdescription VARCHAR2(150), vchreference
VARCHAR2(25), amount NUMBER(15,2))
```

© Riaz Ahmed 2019
R. Ahmed, *Cloud Computing Using Oracle Application Express*,
https://doi.org/10.1007/978-1-4842-4243-8_22

22.2 Create the Parameters Form

As usual, create a blank page using Table 22-1 that will carry two regions: Parameters and Interactive Report.

Table 22-1. *Parameters Form Attributes*

Action	Attribute	Value
Create Blank Page	Page Number	74
	Name	Bank Reconciliation Report
	Page Mode	Normal
	Breadcrumb	—Do not use breadcrumbs on page—
	Navigation Preference	Identify an existing navigation menu entry for this page.
	Existing Navigation Menu Entry	Reports
Create Region	Title	Bank Reconciliation Report Parameters
	Type	Static Content
	Template	Standard
Create Page Item	Name	P74_BANK
	Type	Select List
	Label	Select a bank
	Region	Bank Reconciliation Report Parameters
	Start New Row	Yes
	Column/Column Span	Automatic
	Label Column Span	2
	Template	Required
	Value Required	Yes

(continued)

Table 22-1. (*continued*)

Action	Attribute	Value
	SQL Query	SELECT coacode|| '-'||coatitle d, coacode r FROM gl_coa WHERE cocode=(select cocode from gl_users where userid=:APP_USER) AND coatype='Bank' ORDER BY coacode
Create Page Item	Name	P74_REPORTDATE
	Type	Date Picker
	Label	As On
	Region	Bank Reconciliation Report Parameters
	Label Column Span	2
	Template	Required
	Value Required	Yes
Create Button	Button Name	Display
	Label	Display
	Region	Bank Reconciliation Report Parameters
	Button Position	Copy
	Action	Submit Page
Create Button	Button Name	Print
	Label	Print
	Region	Bank Reconciliation Report Parameters
	Button Position	Copy
	Action	Submit Page

22.3 Create the Interactive Report

Using Table 22-2, create an Interactive Report to produce the onscreen version of the Reconciliation Report. Just like the Trial Balance Report, this too is based on a SELECT statement that fetches the report of the current user from the table GL_RECONCILE_ REPORT.

The table fetches the corresponding data through a process created in the next section.

Table 22-2. *Interactive Report Attributes*

Action	Attribute	Value
Create Region	Title	Bank Reconciliation Report
	Type	Interactive Report
	Type (under Source)	SQL Query
	SQL Query	SELECT * FROM gl_reconcile_report WHERE userid=:APP_USER ORDER BY srno

22.4 Create the Reconciliation Report Generation Process

Create a process as listed in Table 22-3 to generate the Reconciliation Report.

Table 22-3. *Process Attributes*

Action	Attribute	Value
Create Process	Name	Generate Reconciliation Report
	Type	PL/SQL Code
	PL/SQL Code	Book_Code\Chapter22\Generate Reconciliation Report.txt
	Point	Processing
	Server-side Condition	Request is contained in Value
	Value	Display,Print

22.5 Format the Reconciliation Report

Execute the following steps to format the Interactive Report:

1. Hide the SRNO, USERID, CONAME, REPORTDATE, COACODE, and COATITLE columns.

2. Apply a numeric format mask to the Amount column.

3. Modify column headings and give them suitable names, such as **Period**, **Date**, **Type**, **Number**, **Description**, **Reference**, and **Amount**.

4. Run the Reconciliation Report from the Reports menu, and select the values listed in Table 22-4 in the parameters form.

Table 22-4. *Selecting Parameters*

Parameter	Value
Select a bank	ABN Amro
As On	*Select the date you generated the voucher in Chapter 14.*

5. Create a highlight rule to highlight ledger and bank balances using the two conditions listed in Table 22-5. The two expressions appearing in this table were added to the report table through the PL/SQL process, defined on the previous page.

Table 22-5. *Highlight Rule*

Rule Name	Column	Operator	Expression
Bank's Balance	Description	=	Balance as per bank statement
Ledger Balance	Description	=	Balance as per Ledger

6. Save the report by selecting As Default Report Settings followed by the Primary option.

22.6 Generate the PDF Report

Follow the instructions mentioned in Chapter 14 to create a PDF version of the
Reconciliation Report. Use the monthyear column in the "Group by" screen to group
the report according to diferent financial periods. Look at Figure 22-1 where the two
outstanding transactions are reported separately in their respective months.

22.7 Test Your Work

Run this segment first by keeping the two entries (opening outstanding and current
transaction) as unreconciled and watch the output. Then mark both entries as
reconciled and rerun the report to observe the impact. In the former test, the two
balances ("Balance as per Ledger" and "Balance as per bank statement") will yield
different figures, but when you reconcile both entries, the two should display the same
figure. Figure 22-1 shows the parameters form and the report output.

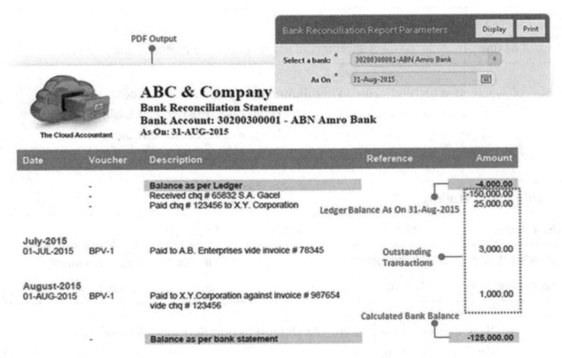

Figure 22-1. *Parameters form and the report output*

22.8 Summary

Bank reconciliation is a monthly activity to keep track of the bank balance and outstanding transactions. The report you created in this chapter reveals both. After completing the interfaces in the previous chapters that deal with the day-to-day accounting tasks, the next couple of chapters deal with the closing process.

CHAPTER 23

Month Closure

It is common practice for organizations to close those fiscal periods for which they are sure to receive no more data. This process is usually referred to as *month closure*. The main purpose of this process is to prevent data manipulation in a closed month. In this chapter, you will create this feature first by creating some procedures to mark a fiscal period as closed and then modifying the main transaction interfaces to apply the desired data security.

23.1 Create Page and Page Items

Using Table 23-1, create a blank page along with its items for this feature. The select list is populated with the 12 fiscal periods of the current company.

Table 23-1. Page Attributes

Action	Attribute	Value
Create Blank Page	Page Number	96
	Name	Month Closure
	Page Mode	Normal
	Breadcrumb	—Do not use breadcrumbs on page—
	Navigation Preference	Identify an existing navigation menu entry for this page.
	Existing Navigation Menu Entry	Closing

(continued)

© Riaz Ahmed 2019
R. Ahmed, *Cloud Computing Using Oracle Application Express*,
https://doi.org/10.1007/978-1-4842-4243-8_23

Table 23-1. (*continued*)

Action	Attribute	Value
Create Region	Title	Month Closure
	Type	Static Content
	Template	Standard
Create Page Item	Name	P96_COMONTH
	Type	Select List
	Label	\Select a month:\
	Page Action on Selection	Submit Page
	Region	Month Closure
	Start New Row	Yes
	Column/Column Span	Automatic
	Label Column Span	2
	Template	Required
	Value Required	Yes
	Type (LOV)	SQL Query

	SQL Query	SELECT comonthname d, comonthid r
		FROM gl_fiscal_year
		WHERE cocode= (select cocode from
		        gl_users where
		        upper(userid)=
		        upper(:APP_USER))
		        AND
		   coyear= (select coyear from
		        gl_users where
		        upper(userid)=
		        upper(:APP_USER))
		ORDER BY comonthid

(*continued*)

Table 23-1. (*continued*)

Action	Attribute	Value
Create Button	Button Name	Close_Month
	Label	Close Month
	Region	Month Closure
	Button Position	Copy
	Action	Submit Page

23.2 Show Unverified Vouchers

Using Table 23-2, add an Interactive Report region to display a list of unverified vouchers. It is being added as a precautionary measure to inform the user about the vouchers that are unverified in the system prior to executing the month closure process. It is good practice to verify all vouchers before closing a month, because vouchers cannot be modified after the month has been closed.

Table 23-2. *Interactive Report Region Attributes*

Action	Attribute	Value
Create Region	Title	Unverified Vouchers
	Type	Interactive Report
	Type (under Source)	SQL Query
	SQL Query	SELECT VCH.vchtype, TM.vchdate, TM.vchno, TM.vchdescription
		FROM gl_voucher VCH, gl_tran_master TM
		WHERE **vchverified='N'** AND VCH.vchcode=TM. vchcode AND
		cocode=(select cocode from gl_users where upper(userid)=upper (:APP_USER)) AND
		coyear=(select coyear from gl_users where upper(userid)=upper (:APP_USER)) AND
		comonthid=:P96_COMONTH

Add meaningful headings to the report's columns, as shown in Figure 23-1. Run the page from the Month Closing option in the main menu. Select the first month (July) from the select list. You'll see the payment voucher you created in Chapter 14, if it is still unverified.

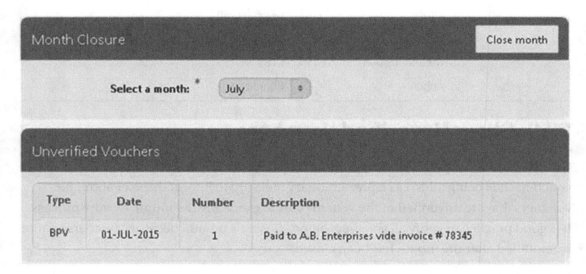

Figure 23-1. *Unverified payment voucher*

23.3 Add Validation

Create the validation listed in Table 23-3 to check whether the selected month is not already closed.

Table 23-3. *Validation Attributes*

Action	Attribute	Value
Create Validation	Name	Check Month Closure
	Type	PL/SQL Function (returning Error Text)
	PL/SQL Function	Book_Code\Chapter23\Check Month Closure.txt
	When Button Pressed	Close_Month

23.4 Close Month Process

The process in Table 23-4 will mark the selected month as closed.

Table 23-4. *Process Attributes*

Action	Attribute	Value
Create Process	Name	⌐Close Month
	Type	PL/SQL Code
	PL/SQL Code	UPDATE gl_fiscal_year SET month_closed=1
		WHERE cocode=(select cocode from gl_users where upper(userid) = upper(:APP_USER)) AND
		coyear= (select coyear from gl_users where upper(userid) = upper(:APP_USER)) AND
		comonthid=:P96_COMONTH;
	Point	Processing
	Success Message	Month closed successfully
	Error Message	Could not close the selected month
	When Button Pressed	Close_Month

Rerun the segment and click the Close Month button. You should see the success message. Click the button again. This time you'll get a message: "Cannot proceed with this process because the selected month is already marked as closed." The message confirms that the month has been marked as closed.

23.5 Hide Buttons

After marking a month as closed, no one is allowed to manipulate data in that month. Implement this security by following the instructions in Tables 23-5 to 23-7. The first one will hide the CREATE button on page 42 (if the month is marked as closed) to disallow the creation of new vouchers. Edit page 42 (Vouchers) and add the hidden item in Table 23-5, which stores the closing status of the current month.

Table 23-5. *Item and Button Attributes*

Action	Attribute	Value
Create Page Item	Name	P42_MONTHCLOSED
	Type	Hidden
	Value Protected	Yes (default)
	Sequence	35 (*to place it after P42_COMONTHID*)
	Region	Vouchers
	Source Type	SQL Query (return single value)
	SQL Query	SELECT month_closed FROM gl_fiscal_year WHERE cocode=(select cocode from gl_users where upper(userid)=upper (:APP_USER)) AND coyear=(select coyear from gl_users where upper(userid)=upper (:APP_USER)) AND comonthid=(select comonthid from gl_users where upper(userid)=upper(:APP_USER))
	Source Used	Always, replacing any existing value in session state

(*continued*)

Table 23-5. (*continued*)

Action	Attribute	Value
Modify Button	Button Name	CREATE
	Server-side Condition	Item = Value
	Item	P42_MONTHCLOSED
	Value	0 (*the button will be visible only when the value of P42_MONTHCLOSED is zero*)

If you run the Vouchers page now, you won't see the CREATE button, which means that the users cannot create a new voucher in a closed month. In the same way, you also have to hide three more buttons on the Voucher Details page (page 43). These are DELETE, SAVE, and CREATE. Table 23-6 shows the procedure to prevent amendments on page 43.

Table 23-6. *Preventing Amendments*

Action	Attribute	Value
Create Page Item	Name	P43_MONTHCLOSED
	Type	Hidden
	Value Protected	Yes (default)
	Region	Enter Voucher
	Source Type	SQL Query (return single value)
	SQL Query	Repeat the query specified for P42_MONTHCLOSED item
	Source Used	Always, replacing any existing value in session state

Now modify the PL/SQL function defined as a condition for the three buttons, as shown in Table 23-7.

Table 23-7. *PL/SQL Function Modifications*

Action	Attribute	Value
Modify Buttons	Button Name	DELETE, SAVE, and CREATE

	PL/SQL Function Body (under Condition)	begin
		  if:P43_TRAN_NO IS NOT NULL and
		    :P43_CLOSING=0 and
		    :P43_VCHVERIFIED='N' **and :P43_**
		    MONTHCLOSED=0 then
		    return true;
		  else
		    return false;
		  end if;
		end;

23.6 Summary

After executing the month closing process, users cannot add, modify, or delete any voucher in a closed month. This way, the historical data is protected from any kind of manipulation. In the next chapter, you will create two year-end processes to close a fiscal year either temporarily or permanently.

CHAPTER 24

Year-End Processes

The year-end process consists of two options: temporary and permanent. The temporary year-end process performs two actions: first, it generates the next fiscal year, and then it transfers the balances of accounts from the closing year to the new fiscal year. When you select this option from the Closing menu, the system asks you to provide a profit and loss account from the chart of accounts (COA), which is used to transfer the difference of revenues and expenses.

The second option is the permanent year-end process, which has two additional tasks: first, it checks the closure status of the 12 fiscal periods, and then it marks the year as permanently closed. After the successful completion of this process, you can view the transactions performed in that year and generate reports, but you cannot add, amend, or delete anything.

24.1 Enter Opening Balances

If you are running a business, then you will have some accounts with balances. When you upgrade your general ledger application, these balances act as opening balances in the new application. In this section, you'll incorporate these balances in your application to test the year-end process. It is assumed that you have created a fiscal year (2015) for the ABC & Company, which starts from July 1, 2015, and ends June 30, 2016. From the Select menu, change your working period to June—in other words, the last accounting period. Enter the opening balances of accounts in a JV type voucher using Table 24-1.

© Riaz Ahmed 2019
R. Ahmed, *Cloud Computing Using Oracle Application Express*,
https://doi.org/10.1007/978-1-4842-4243-8_24

Table 24-1. *Opening Balances of Accounts*

Voucher Type: ADJ	Voucher Number: 1		Voucher Date: 30-JUN-2016		

Description: Opening Balances

Account Code	Account Title	Description	Debit	Credit
10100100001	M.H. Thomson	Opening Balance		50,000
10100100002	A.F. Stevens	Opening Balance		50,000
10100300001	Unappropriate Profit/Loss	Opening Balance	20,500	
20100100001	A.B. Enterprises	Opening Balance	10,000	
20100100002	X.Y. Corporation	Opening Balance		40,000
20100200001	Salaries Payable	Opening Balance		8,000
20100200002	Utilities Payable	Opening Balance		4,000
20100300001	ABN Amro Bank (STF)	Opening Balance		12,000
20100400002	Caponi SRL	Opening Balance	6,000	
20100400001	HNH International	Opening Balance		3,000
20100500001	Motor Car (AD)	Opening Balance		4,500
20100500002	Delivery Truck (AD)	Opening Balance		5,000
20200200001	Staff Gratuity Payable	Opening Balance		20,000
30100100001	Office Building	Opening Balance	100,000	
30100100002	Warehouse	Opening Balance	100,000	
30100200002	Computers	Opening Balance	10,000	
30100300001	Motor Car	Opening Balance	30,000	
30200100001	Stock - Raw Material	Opening Balance	1,000	
30200200001	S.A. Gacel	Opening Balance	2,000	
30200200002	B.V.Heliform	Opening Balance		100,000
30200300001	ABN Amro Bank	Opening Balance	150,000	

(continued)

Table 24-1. (*continued*)

Account Code	Account Title	Description	Debit	Credit
40100100001	Export Sales	Opening Balance		175,000
50100100001	Stock Consumption—Raw Material	Opening Balance	15,000	
50200100001	Staff Salaries Expense (Admin)	Opening Balance	8,000	
50200100002	Gratuity Expense	Opening Balance	12,000	
50200200001	Electricity Expense	Opening Balance	1,500	
50200300001	Depreciation—Motor Car	Opening Balance	2,000	
50300200001	Depreciation Expense—Delivery Truck	Opening Balance	3,500	
Total			**471,500**	**471,500**

24.2 Temporary Year-End (TYE)

Up until now you have created each application feature in a separate chapter. Though the two year-end segments are listed individually under the Closing menu, you will create both of them in this chapter. Perform the following steps to first create the temporary year-end (TYE) segment.

24.3 Create the Page and Page Items

The TYE process will receive two values from the user: Voucher Type and Profit and Loss Account. This closing process will first create a new fiscal year. If one already exists, for example, you execute this process for a second time, this step will be skipped. After creating the new fiscal year, the year-end process generates a closing voucher of the selected type to close all revenues and expenses into an account called the Profit and Loss Account. For this purpose, the segment receives the two parameters mentioned earlier. Create a new blank page with page items in Table 24-2.

Table 24-2. *Page Attributes*

Action	Attribute	Value
Create Blank Page	Page Number	93
	Name	Temporary Year-End
	Page Mode	Normal
	Breadcrumb	—Do not use breadcrumbs on page—
	Navigation Preference	Identify an existing navigation menu entry for this page.
	Existing Navigation Menu Entry	Closing
Create Region	Title	Temporary Year-End
	Type	Static Content
	Template	Standard
Create Page Item	Name	P93_VCHCODE
	Type	Select List
	Label	Select a voucher type:
	Region	Temporary Year-End
	Label Column Span	2
	Template	Required
	Value Required	Yes
	LOV Type	Shared Component
	List of Values	VOUCHER TYPES
Create Page Item	Name	P93_PLACCOUNT
	Type	Popup LOV
	Label	P&L Account:
	Region	Temporary Year-End
	Label Column Span	2
	Template	Required

(continued)

Table 24-2. (*continued*)

Action	Attribute	Value
	Value Required	Yes
	LOV Type	Shared Component
	List of Values	COA Entry Level
Create Button	Button Name	GO
	Label	Execute TYE
	Region	Temporary Year-End
	Button Position	Copy
	Action	Submit Page

24.4 Create a Validation

Add the validation in Table 24-3 to check that the current year is not permanently closed. In such a case, the TYE process will not execute.

Table 24-3. *Validation Attributes*

Action	Attribute	Value
Create Validation	Name	Check Permanent Year Closure
	Type	PL/SQL Function (returning Error Text)
	PL/SQL Function	Book_Code\Chapter24\Check Permanent Year Closure.txt
	When Button Pressed	GO

24.5 Generate the Fiscal Year Process

The process in Table 24-4 creates a new fiscal year when you execute the TYE process for the first time.

Table 24-4. *Process Attributes*

Action	Attribute	Value
Create Process	Name	Generate Fiscal Year
	Type	PL/SQL Code
	PL/SQL Code	Book_Code\Chapter24\Generate Fiscal Year.txt
	Point	Processing
	When Button Pressed	GO

24.6 A Process to Generate a Closing Entry

The process in Table 24-5 will close all revenue and expense accounts into a profit and loss account that you will select as the second parameter.

Table 24-5. *Process Attributes*

Action	Attribute	Value
Create Process	Name	Generate Closing Entry
	Type	PL/SQL Code
	PL/SQL Code	Book_Code\Chapter24\Generate Closing Entry.txt
	Point	Processing
	Success Message	Temporary year-end process executed successfully.
	Error Message	Could not execute the TYE process.
	When Button Pressed	GO

> **Note**   The TYE process must be executed to update the profit and loss account whenever you manipulate data in the previous fiscal year.

24.7 Test Your Work

Invoke the page from the TYE option in the Closing menu, as shown in Figure 24-1. Select a JV type voucher from the first drop-down list. For the second parameter, select the account titled "Unappropriated Profit/Loss account" from the chart of accounts and click the Execute TYE button. You should see a success message after the execution of the process. Now click the Transactions menu and select the voucher type you chose to store the closing entry. You'll see two vouchers in the vouchers report list. The first voucher is the one you entered through Table 24-1 to record opening balances, while the second (numbered 9999999999) is created by the TYE process to close expense and revenue accounts. Note that this voucher is marked as both verified and posted, which means you cannot modify or delete its contents. Click the edit link next to it and notice that all the data manipulation buttons have disappeared from the details page. The only button you should see is the Cancel button that takes you back to the reports page. Also note that the closing voucher is reflected in the Ledger Report in the year it was created. For example, if you run a Ledger Report for an expense or a revenue account, you'll see this voucher. The first task that this process performed was the creation of a new fiscal year. To verify this, click the Select menu and expand the Year select list. Now there will be two years: 2015 and 2016.

24.8 Permanent Year End (PYE)

This is the second year-end process, which prevents any kind of data manipulation operation in a year marked as permanently closed. Execute the following sections to create this process.

24.9 Create the Page and Page Items

Using Table 24-6, create a blank page and items to create the permanent year-end (PYE) process.

Table 24-6. *Page Attributes*

Action	Attribute	Value
Create Blank Page	Page Number	97
	Name	Permanent Year-End
	Page Mode	Normal
	Breadcrumb	—Do not use breadcrumbs on page—
	Navigation Preference	Identify an existing navigation menu entry for this page.
	Existing Navigation Menu Entry	Closing
Create Region	Title	Permanent Year-End
	Type	Static Content
	Text	<p> Before you proceed, make sure that: You have closed all 12 fiscal periods.
		You have executed Temporary Year End process recently to register latest closing entries.
		Click Go to proceed!</p>
	Template	Standard
Create Button	Button Name	GO
	Label	GO
	Region	Permanent Year-End
	Button Position	Copy
	Action	Submit Page

24.10 Create the Validations

Create the validations in Table 24-7 to fully execute the PYE process. The first validation checks whether the current year is not already marked as permanently closed. For this process to be successful, it is necessary to first close all 12 periods. The second validation ensures that all 12 fiscal periods have been marked as closed. The final validation needs you to execute the TYE process to record the latest closing entries.

Table 24-7. *Validation Attributes*

Action	Attribute	Value
Create Validation	Name	Permanent Year Closure
	Type	PL/SQL Function (returning Error Text)
	PL/SQL Function	Book_Code\Chapter24\Permanent Year Closure.txt
	When Button Pressed	GO
Create Validation	Name	Check Months Closure
	Type	PL/SQL Function (returning Error Text)
	PL/SQL Function	Book_Code\Chapter24\Check Months Closure.txt
	When Button Pressed	GO
Create Validation	Name	Check Temporary Year End Date
	Type	PL/SQL Function (returning Error Text)
	PL/SQL Function	Book_Code\Chapter24\Check Temporary Year End Date.txt
	When Button Pressed	GO

24.11 A Process to Close the Year Permanently

After passing the validations, the currently selected year is marked as permanently closed by the process mentioned in Table 24-8.

Table 24-8. *Process Attributes*

Action	Attribute	Value
Create Process	Name	Close Year Permanently
	Type	PL/SQL Code
	PL/SQL Code	UPDATE gl_fiscal_year SET year_closed=1 WHERE cocode=(select cocode from gl_users where upper(userid) = upper (:APP_USER)) and coyear=(select coyear from gl_users where upper(userid) = upper (:APP_USER));
	Point	Processing
	Success Message	Permanent year-end process executed successfully.
	Error Message	Could not execute the PYE process.
	When Button Pressed	GO

24.12 Test Your Work

Run the Permanent Year-End segment from the Closing menu; you will see the PYE page, as illustrated in Figure 24-1. Hit the Go button. The process will not execute because the 12 fiscal periods are open and must be marked as closed prior to executing this process. Do so by closing all the periods individually from the Month Closing option under the Closing menu and execute this process again. If you ran the TYE process on the same date, the PYE process should execute successfully in this attempt; otherwise, you will get another message to execute the TYE process to register fresh closing entries. After successful execution of this process, transaction manipulation actions are permanently prevented in the current year. Of course, you can view the data through the voucher interface and the reports.

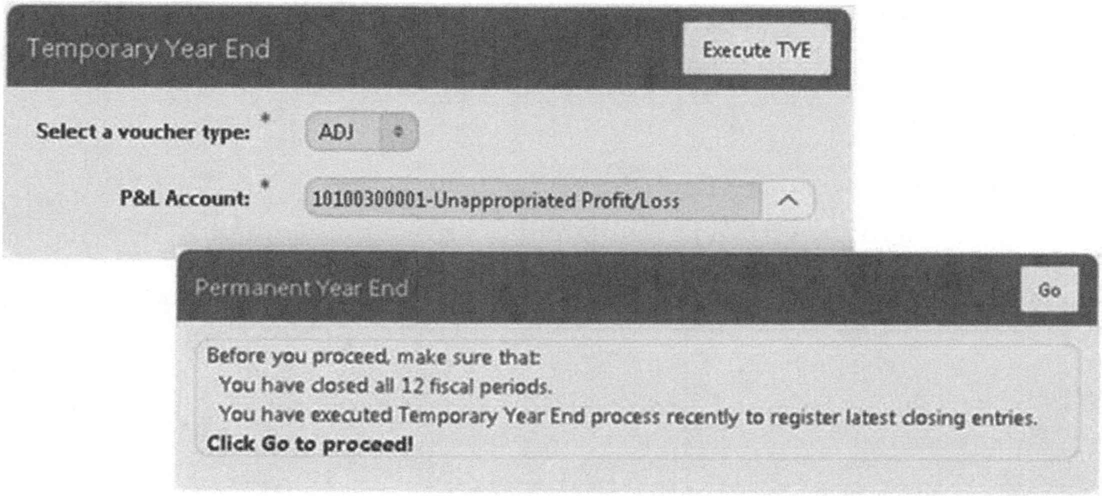

Figure 24-1. *Year-end pages*

24.13 Summary

After executing the TYE process, you get the next fiscal year. Also, the closing balances of assets, liabilities, and capital accounts are transferred to the next fiscal year. In the next couple of chapters, you will learn how to develop a budget module.

CHAPTER 25

Budget Allocation

A budget is a useful tool to keep spending under control. Every good organization uses this tool to keep an eye on its activities. After allocating a budget to an account, it is compared to the actual expenditure to make sure there is no overspend of money. In the initial year, budgets are allocated manually because of the absence of historical data. In subsequent years, you have two options to define budgets: you can reuse last year's budget or allocate last year's actual spend to act as the current year's budget.

25.1 Budget Allocation Table

Budgets will be saved in the following table for each company, year, and account:

```
CREATE TABLE gl_budget
(cocode number constraint fk_budget1 References GL_Company (Cocode)
NOT NULL, coyear number(4), coacode varchar2(11) NOT NULL, coanature
varchar2(11) NOT NULL, cccode varchar2(5), budget_amount1 number(15,2),
budget_amount2 number(15,2), budget_amount3 number(15,2), budget_amount4
number(15,2), budget_amount5 number(15,2), budget_amount6 number(15,2),
budget_amount7 number(15,2), budget_amount8 number(15,2), budget_amount9
number(15,2), budget_amount10 number(15,2), budget_amount11 number(15,2),
budget_amount12 number(15,2), criterion number(1), constraint fk_budget2
Foreign Key (cocode,coacode) References GL_COA);
```

25.2 Create the Page and Parameters Form

Using Table 25-1, create a blank page and add components to it. The two hidden items defined underneath will store the current company's code and year to properly save the budget. Budgets are mainly allocated according to the nature of the account, so you also add a select list to display the five natures from the chart of accounts (COA).

261

© Riaz Ahmed 2019
R. Ahmed, *Cloud Computing Using Oracle Application Express*,
https://doi.org/10.1007/978-1-4842-4243-8_25

Table 25-1. *Page Attributes*

Action	Attribute	Value
Create Blank Page	Page Number	55
	Name	Budget Allocation
	Page Mode	Normal
	Navigation Preference	Identify an existing navigation menu entry for this page.
	Existing Navigation Menu Entry	Utilities
Create Region	Title	Budget Allocation Parameters
	Type	Static Content
	Template	Standard
Create Page Item	Name	P55_COCODE
	Type	Hidden
	Source Type	SQL Query (return single value)
	SQL Query	SELECT cocode FROM gl_users WHERE userid = :app_user
	Source Used	Always, replacing any existing value in session state
Create Page Item	Name	P55_COYEAR
	Type	Hidden
	Source Type	SQL Query (return single value)
	SQL Query	SELECT coyear FROM gl_users WHERE userid = :app_user
	Source Used	Always, replacing any existing value in session state

(continued)

Table 25-1. (*continued*)

Action	Attribute	Value
Create Page Item	Name	P55_COANATURE
	Type	Select List
	Label	Nature of Account:
	Page Action on Selection	Submit Page
	Region	Budget Allocation Parameters
	Start New Row	Yes
	Column/Column Span	Automatic
	Label Column Span	2
	Template	Required
	Value Required	Yes
	LOV Type	SQL Query
	SQL Query	SELECT DISTINCT coanature d, coanature r FROM gl_coa WHERE cocode= (select cocode from gl_users where userid=:APP_USER)

The three options defined in the Radio Group page item (Table 25-2) help users evaluate which type of budget was saved for the selected nature of account. For example, if a budget was created for a particular nature using the first option (User Defined), then whenever the user selects that nature, the first type is highlighted. After selecting an account nature, you click one of the three provided buttons (User Defined, Last Year Budget, or Last Year Actual in Table 25-2) to specify what type of budget you want to allocate. These buttons are associated with respective processes defined using Table 25-5 later in the chapter.

Table 25-2. *Item and Button Attributes*

Action	Attribute	Value
Create Page Item	Name	P55_CRITERIA
	Type	Radio Group
	Label	Type of Budget:
	Number of Columns	3
	Region	Budget Allocation Parameters
	Start New Row	Yes
	Column/Column Span	Automatic
	Label Column Span	2
	LOV Type	Static Values
	Static Values	STATIC:1-User Defined;1,2-Last Year Budget;2, 3-Last Year Actual;3
	Display Null Value	No
	Source Type	SQL Query (return single value)
	SQL Query	SELECT DISTINCT criterion FROM gl_budget WHERE cocode=:P55_COCODE AND coyear=:P55_COYEAR AND coanature=:P55_COANATURE
	Source Used	Always, replacing any existing value in session state
	Default Type	Static Value
	Static Value	1
Create Button	Name	User_Defined
	Label	User Defined
	Region	Budget Allocation Parameters
	Position	Copy
	Action	Submit Page

(*continued*)

Table 25-2. (*continued*)

Action	Attribute	Value
Create Button	Name	Last_Year_Budget
	Label	Last Year Budget
	Region	Budget Allocation Parameters
	Position	Copy
	Action	Submit Page
Create Button	Name	Last_Year_Actual
	Label	Last Year Actual
	Region	Budget Allocation Parameters
	Position	Copy
	Action	Submit Page

25.3 Add an Interactive Grid

After selecting an account nature, you click one of the three buttons created in the previous section. The processes associated with these buttons execute and populate the table GL_BUDGET with respective accounts and values. To browse the result and to manipulate the values, you need to create an Interactive Grid. Create a new page. Select Form followed by Editable Interactive Grid. Use Table 25-3 to set attributes for this page.

Table 25-3. *Tabular Form Region*

Action	Attribute	Value
Create Page	Page Number	55
	Page Name	Allocate Budget
	Page Mode	Normal
	Existing Navigation Menu Entry	Utilities
	Source Type	Table
	Table Name	GL_BUDGET
	Primary Key	ROWID
	Select Columns	Select all columns

After creation, enter **Allocate budget for &P55_COANATURE. Accounts** for the region title.

Modify the new Interactive Grid region to incorporate the following amendments:

1. Add a WHERE clause to the region's SQL query as follows to display the data of the current company, year, and selected nature:

```
SELECT "ROWID","COCODE","COYEAR","COACODE","COANATURE",
       "CCCODE","BUDGET_AMOUNT1",
       "BUDGET_AMOUNT2","BUDGET_AMOUNT3","BUDGET_AMOUNT4",
       "BUDGET_AMOUNT5",
       "BUDGET_AMOUNT6","BUDGET_AMOUNT7","BUDGET_AMOUNT8",
       "BUDGET_AMOUNT9",
       "BUDGET_AMOUNT10","BUDGET_AMOUNT11","BUDGET_
       AMOUNT12","CRITERION"
FROM   "#OWNER#"."GL_BUDGET"
WHERE cocode=:P55_COCODE and coyear=:P55_COYEAR and
      coanature=:P55_COANATURE
```

2. Modify the attributes listed in Table 25-4 for the COACODE column.

Table 25-4. *COACODE Attributes*

Attribute	Value
Type	Popup LOV
Heading	Account
LOV Type	Shared Component
List of Values	COA ENTRY LEVEL

3. Set the Type attribute to Hidden for the COCODE, COYEAR, COANATURE, CCCODE, and CRITERION columns.

4. Modify the COCODE column. Set its Default Type value to **Item** and enter **P55_COCODE** in the Item attribute. Repeat the same for the COYEAR (P55_COYEAR), COANATURE (P55_COANATURE),

and CRITERION (P55_CRITERIA) columns. This way, the four table columns will inherit values from the corresponding page items.

5. Set headings for the 12 Budget Amount columns as Month 1, Month 2, and so on, as shown in Figure 25-1 later in this chapter.

25.4 Budget Processes

Using Table 25-5, add three processes to handle the allocation. Each process is associated with a particular button to populate the GL_BUDGET table.

Table 25-5. *Process Attributes*

Action	Attribute	Value
Create Process	Name	User-Defined Budget
	Type	PL/SQL Code
	PL/SQL Code	Book_Code\Chapter25\User Defined Budget.txt
	Point	Processing
	When Button Pressed	User_Defined
Create Process	Name	Last Year Budget
	Type	PL/SQL Code
	PL/SQL Code	Book_Code\Chapter25\Last Year Budget.txt
	Point	Processing
	When Button Pressed	Last_Year_Budget
Create Process	Name	Last Year Actual
	Type	PL/SQL Code
	PL/SQL Code	Book_Code\Chapter25\Last Year Actual.txt
	Point	Processing
	When Button Pressed	Last_Year_Actual

25.5 Test Your Work

Budgets are usually applied to expenses to keep them under control. However, the segment created in this chapter can be used to set a budget for any nature of account. Let's see how a budget is defined.

1. Now that you have two fiscal years (2015 and 2016) for ABC & Company, switch to the new fiscal year (2016) from the select menu. Selecting a period is not necessary for this segment.

2. Invoke the Budget Allocation segment from the Utilities menu.

3. Set Nature of Account to Assets and click the User Defined button. The process associated with this button will populate the tabular form with all asset accounts from the COA. Note that the first month column (Month 1) represents the first month of the fiscal year. In the current scenario, the first month represents July, the second month represents August, and so on. Enter some numeric figures in some month columns for different accounts and click the Apply Changes button to save the budget values. Switch the nature of account to some other nature and then back to the Assets nature. You'll see the saved figures. Also, note that the type of budget is set to the first option—in other words, User Defined. You save the budget using the Apply Changes button only when you define it manually. For the other two options, you are not required to use this button unless you change the fetched values or add/delete rows from the tabular form.

4. Select Expenses as the nature of account and hit the Last Year Actual button, as shown at the top of Figure 25-1. Scroll to extreme right and note the figures being shown in the Month 12 column, as shown at the bottom of Figure 25-1. These are the figures that you entered as opening balances for respective expense accounts in the month of June in the previous fiscal year.

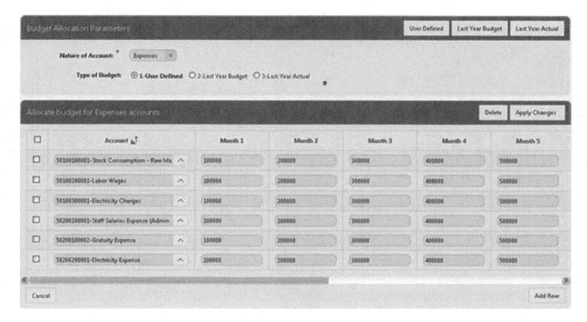

Figure 25-1. *Budget allocation page*

25.6 Summary

Since you do not have any previous year budget data, you won't get any result if you click the Last Year Budget button. For this, you will have to create another fiscal year using the temporary year-end process, and then you can use the budget you set in the previous steps. The next chapter provides instructions to generate a Budget Report.

CHAPTER 26

Budget Report

The Budget Report displays the variance between the allocated budget figure and the actual figure recorded through vouchers. It also carries a Status column to signify whether the actual value exceeded (over-applied: O) the allocated budget or it remained within the defined limit (under-applied: U). The parameters form allows you to generate this report for a particular nature, for a single account or a range of accounts, and for different durations.

26.1 Budget Report Table

The following table (already created through the script file) stores Budget Report values generated by a process defined in Table 26-5 later in the chapter.

```
CREATE TABLE gl_budget_report
(coacode VARCHAR2(11), coatitle VARCHAR2(50), budget NUMBER(15,2),
actual NUMBER(15,2), variance NUMBER(15,2), percent NUMBER(7,2),
status VARCHAR2(1), userid VARCHAR2(50), grand_total NUMBER(1), coname
VARCHAR2(50), AccountFrom VARCHAR2(11), AccountTo VARCHAR2(11), MonthFrom
VARCHAR2(9), MonthTo VARCHAR2(9),
PrintedOn timestamp)
```

26.2 Create Page and Parameters Form

As usual, create a blank page (using Table 26-1) that will carry two regions: Parameters and Interactive Report. By selecting an option from the Nature radio group list, you apply a filter to display accounts associated with the selected nature in the two LOVs defined on the next page.

271

© Riaz Ahmed 2019
R. Ahmed, *Cloud Computing Using Oracle Application Express*,
https://doi.org/10.1007/978-1-4842-4243-8_26

Table 26-1. *Page Attributes*

Action	Attribute	Value
Create Blank Page	Page Number	75
	Name	Budget Report
	Page Mode	Normal
	Breadcrumb	—Do not use breadcrumbs on page—
	Navigation Preference	Identify an existing navigation menu entry for this page.
	Existing Navigation Menu Entry	Reports
Create Region	Title	Budget Report Parameters
	Type	Static Content
	Template	Standard
Create Page Item	Name	P75_COANATUR
	Type	Radio Group
	Label	Nature:
	Number of Columns	6
	Page Action on Selection	Submit Page
	Region	Budget Report Parameters
	Start New Row	Yes
	Column/Column Span	Automatic
	Label Column Span	2
	Type (LOV)	Static Values
	Static Values	STATIC:Capital;Capital,Liabilities;Liabilities,Assets; Assets, Expenses;Expenses,Revenue;Reve nue
	Display Null Value	No
	Type (Default)	Static Value
	Static Value	Revenue

(continued)

Table 26-1. (*continued*)

Action	Attribute	Value
Create Page Item	Name	P75_ACCOUNTFROM
	Type	Popup LOV
	Label	From:
	Region	Budget Report Parameters
	Label Column Span	2
	Template	Required
	Value Required	Yes
	LOV Type	SQL Query

	SQL Query	SELECT coacode||'-'||coatitle d,
		    coacode r FROM gl_coa
		WHERE cocode=(select cocode from
		    gl_users
		    where userid=:APP_
		    USER) AND
		  coalevel=4 AND
		  coanature=:P75_COANATURE
		ORDER BY coacode

Create Page Item	Name	P75_ACCOUNTTO
	Type	Popup LOV
	Label	To:
	Region	Budget Report Parameters
	Label Column Span	2
	Template	Required
	Value Required	Yes
	LOV Type	SQL Query
	SQL Query	*Same as the one defined for P75_ACCOUNTFROM*

(*continued*)

Table 26-1. (*continued*)

Action	Attribute	Value
Create Page Item	Name	P75_MONTHFROM
	Type	Select List
	Label	From:
	Region	Budget Report Parameters
	Start New Row	Yes
	Column/Column Span	Automatic
	Label Column Span	2
	Template	Required
	Value Required	Yes
	LOV Type	SQL Query
	SQL Query	SELECT comonthname d,comonthid r FROM gl_fiscal_year WHERE cocode=(select cocode from gl_users where userid=:APP_USER) AND coyear=(select coyear from gl_users where userid=:APP_USER) ORDER BY comonthid
	Default Type	Static Value
	Static Value	1

(*continued*)

Table 26-1. (*continued*)

Action	Attribute	Value
Create Page Item	Name	P75_MONTHTO
	Type	Select List
	Label	To:
	Region	Budget Report Parameters
	Start New Row	Yes
	Column/Column Span	Automatic
	Label Column Span	2
	Template	Required
	Value Required	Yes
	LOV Type	SQL Query
	SQL Query	*Same as the one defined for P75_MONTHFROM*
	Default Type	Static Value
	Static Value	1
Create Page Item	Name	P75_COCODE
	Type	Hidden
	Region	Budget Report Parameters
	Source Type	SQL Query (return single value)
	SQL Query	SELECT cocode FROM gl_users WHERE userid=:APP_USER
	Source Used	Always, replacing any existing value in session state

(*continued*)

Table 26-1. (*continued*)

Action	Attribute	Value
Create Page Item	Name	P75_COCODE
	Type	Hidden
	Region	Budget Report Parameters
	Source Type	SQL Query (return single value)
	SQL Query	SELECT cocode FROM gl_users WHERE userid=:APP_USER
	Source Used	Always, replacing any existing value in session state
Create Page Item	Name	P75_COYEAR
	Type	Hidden
	Region	Budget Report Parameters
	Source Type	SQL Query (return single value)
	SQL Query	SELECT coyear FROM gl_users WHERE userid=:APP_USER
	Source Used	Always, replacing any existing value in session state
Create Button	Button Name	Display
	Label	Display
	Region	Budget Report Parameters
	Button Position	Copy
	Action	Submit Page
Create Button	Button Name	Print
	Label	Print
	Region	Budget Report Parameters
	Button Position	Copy
	Action	Submit Page

26.3 Create Computations

On the Rendering tab, expand the Pre-Rendering node to create two computations (listed in Table 26-2) to display the first and last accounts from the chart of accounts (COA) in the corresponding page items. Right-click the Before Header node and select Create Computation from the context menu. This will add a Computations node under the Before Header node. Set the following attributes as shown in Table 26-2.

Table 26-2. *Computation Attributes*

Action	Attribute	Value
Create Computation	Item Name	P75_ACCOUNTFROM
	Point	Before Header
	Computation Type	SQL Query (return single value)
	SQL Query	SELECT **MIN(coacode)** FROM gl_coa WHERE coanature=:P75_COANATURE AND coalevel=4 AND cocode=:P75_COCODE
Create Computation	Item Name	P75_ACCOUNTTO
	Point	Before Header
	Computation Type	SQL Query (return single value)
	SQL Query	SELECT **MAX(coacode)** FROM gl_coa WHERE coanature=:P75_COANATURE AND coalevel=4 AND cocode=:P75_COCODE

26.4 Create Interactive Report

Using Table 26-3, create an Interactive Report to create the onscreen version of the Budget Report.

Table 26-3. *Interactive Report Attributes*

Action	Attribute	Value
Create Region	Title	Budget Report
	Type	Interactive Report
	SQL Query	SELECT * FROM gl_budget_report WHERE userid=:APP_USER ORDER BY grand_total,coacode
	Template	Standard

Modify the Interactive Report to incorporate the following amendments:

1. Set meaningful column headings.

2. Run the page, and using the Actions menu ➤ Select Columns option, move Account Code, Title, Budgeted Amount, Actual Amount, Variance, Percent, and Status columns to the Display in Report pane.

3. Create a highlight rule as listed in Table 26-4 to highlight the grand total row using different text and background colors.

Table 26-4. *Highlight Rule*

Rule Name	Column	Operator	Expression
Grand Total	Grand Total	=	1

4. Save the report by selecting As Default Report Settings, followed by the Primary option.

26.5 Budget Report Generation Process

The process mentioned in Table 26-5 generates the Budget Report and stores the result in the gl_budget_report table with respective user ID and parameters.

Table 26-5. *Budget Report Generation Process*

Action	Attribute	Value
Create Process	Name	Generate Budget Report
	Type	PL/SQL Code
	PL/SQL Code	Book_Code\Chapter26\Generate Budget Report.txt
	Point	Processing
	Server-side Condition	Request is contained in value
	Value	Display,Print

26.6 Test Your Work

Execute the following steps to test this segment. Make sure your current company is ABC & Company and your working period is July 2016. In other words, the text *ABC & Company July, 2016* should display on your screen.

1. Using Tables 26-6 and 26-7, create two sales vouchers. Note that I created a separate voucher type (SI) to record sales transactions.

Table 26-6. *Sales Voucher 1*

Voucher Type: SI	Voucher Number: 1		Voucher Date: 01-JUL-2016	

Description: Recorded export sales vide invoice # 123456

Account Code	Account Title	Description	Debit	Credit
30200200001	S.A. Gacel	Recorded export sales vide invoice # 123456	100,000	-
40100100001	Export Sales	Recorded export sales vide invoice # 123456	-	100,000
Total			**100,000**	**100,000**

Table 26-7. *Sales Voucher 2*

Voucher Type: SI	Voucher Number: 2	Voucher Date: 15-JUL-2016

Description: Recorded local sales vide invoice # 987654

Account Code	Account Title	Description	Debit	Credit
30200200002	B.V. Heliform	Recorded local sales vide invoice # 987654	150,000	-
40100100002	Local Sales	Recorded local sales vide invoice # 987654	-	150,000
Total			**150,000**	**150,000**

2. From the Utilities menu, click the Budget Allocation option. Select Revenue as the nature of account and click the User Defined button. You'll get the four accounts marked as Revenue in the tabular form. Enter **120000** and **100000** in the Month 1 column for Export Sales and Local Sales, respectively. This will set a budget for these two accounts for the month of July. Click the Apply Changes button.

3. Invoke the Budget Report segment from the Reports menu. Fill in the parameters as shown in Figure 26-1 (top) and hit the Display button. You will see the report shown in Figure 26-1 (bottom).

ABC & Company
Budget Report
Printed On: 31-AUG-2015 10:39AM

The Cloud Accountant

From Account:	40100100001		To Account:	40100100002
From:	July		To:	July

Account	Budget	Actual	Variance	Percent	Status
40100100001-Export Sales	120,000.00	100,000	20,000.00	16.67	U
40100100002-Local Sales	100,000.00	150,000	-50,000.00	-50.00	O
GRAND TOTAL	220,000.00	250,000	-30,000.00	-13.64	O

Figure 26-1. *Budget Report*

26.7 Summary

The process of creating a budget takes management away from its short-term, day-to-day management of the business and forces it to think longer-term. It is the most basic and the most effective tool for managing money. After allocating budget in Chapter 25, you created a report in this chapter to keep an eye on your budget allocation. In the next chapter, you will set up foundation for financial statements.

CHAPTER 27

Set Up Accounts for Financial Statements

Organizations prepare financial statements periodically (especially at the end of a fiscal year) to assess business performance. The two most common financial statements are the Profit and Loss (P&L) Statement and the Balance Sheet. In this chapter, you will create a setup where users will provide parameters in the form of account codes from the chart of accounts (COA) for these two reports. These accounts will be used in the next chapter to produce the two financial statements.

27.1 Accounts Table for the Financial Statements

The following table was created through the script file to store financial statement accounts:

```
CREATE TABLE gl_fs_setup
(cocode NUMBER, reportcode varchar2(4), reporttitle varchar2(50), fsaccount
varchar2(50), AccountFrom varchar2(11), AccountTo varchar2(11), CONSTRAINT
GL_FS_SETUP_PK PRIMARY KEY (cocode,reportcode,fsaccount) ENABLE)
```

© Riaz Ahmed 2019
R. Ahmed, *Cloud Computing Using Oracle Application Express,*
https://doi.org/10.1007/978-1-4842-4243-8_27

27.2 Create a List of Values

Using Table 27-1, create a static list of values (LOV) from scratch and name it Financial Statement Accounts.

Table 27-1. *Financial Statement Accounts LOV*

Display Value	Return Value	
Sales	Sales	Profit & Loss Parameters
Cost of Goods	Cost of Goods	
Administrative Expenses	Admin	
Selling & Marketing Expenses	Selling	
Financial Charges	Financial	
Share Capital	Share Capital	Balance Sheet Parameters
Reserves	Reserves	
Profit/(Loss)	Profit/(Loss)	
Trade Creditors	Trade Creditors	
Accrued Expenses	Accrued Expenses	
Short Term Finance	Short Term Finance	
Advance From Customers	Advance From Customers	
Accumulated Depreciation	Accumulated Depreciation	
Banks Overdrafts	Banks Overdrafts	
Long-Term Liabilities	Long-Term Liabilities	
Building	Building	
Office Equipment	Office Equipment	
Vehicles	Vehicles	
Stock in Trade	Stock in Trade	
Trade Debts	Trade Debts	
Cash and Bank	Cash and Bank	

Note   Initially the LOV wizard allows 15 entries. To add more entries, modify the LOV and use the Create Entry button.

27.3 Create Page and Page Items

Create a blank page and add the items to it using Table 27-2.

Table 27-2. *Page Attributes*

Action	Attribute	Value
Create Blank Page	Page Number	18
	Name	Financial Statements Setup
	Page Mode	Normal
	Breadcrumb	—Do not use breadcrumbs on page—
	Navigation Preference	Identify an existing navigation menu entry for this page.
	Existing Navigation Menu Entry	Setup
Create Region	Title	Financial Statements Parameters
	Type	Static Content
	Template	Standard

(*continued*)

Table 27-2. (*continued*)

Action	Attribute	Value
Create Page Item	Name	P18_COCODE
	Type	Hidden
	Region	Financial Statements Parameters
	Source Type	SQL Query (return single value)
	SQL Query	`SELECT cocode FROM gl_users WHERE userid=:APP_USER`
	Source Used	Always, replacing any existing value in session state
Create Page Item	Name	P18_EXISTINGNEW
	Type	Radio Group
	Label	\Report:\
	Number of Columns	2
	Page Action on Selection	Submit Page
	Region	Financial Statements Parameters
	Start New Row	Yes
	Column/Column Span	Automatic
	Label Column Span	2
	Template	Required
	LOV Type	Static Values
	Static Values	STATIC:New;NEW,Existing;EXISTING
	Display Null Value	No
	Type (Default)	Static Value
	Static Value	EXISTING

(*continued*)

Table 27-2. (*continued*)

Action	Attribute	Value
Create Page Item	Name	P18_REPORTCODE1
	Type	Select List
	Label	<b>Code:</b>
	Page Action on Selection	Submit Page
	Region	Financial Statements Parameters
	Start New Row	No
	Column	Automatic
	New Column	Yes
	Column Span	Automatic
	Label Column Span	2
	Template	Required
	Value Required	No
	LOV Type	SQL Query
	SQL Query	SELECT DISTINCT reportcode d, reportcode r FROM gl_fs_setup WHERE cocode=:P18_COCODE
	Server-side Condition	Item = Value
	Item	P18_EXISTINGNEW
	Value	EXISTING

(continued)

Table 27-2. (*continued*)

Action	Attribute	Value
Create Page Item	Name	P18_REPORTTITLE1
	Type	Text Field
	Label	Title:
	Region	Financial Statements Parameters
	Start New Row	No
	Column	Automatic
	New Column	Yes
	Column Span	Automatic
	Label Column Span	2
	Width	50
	Source Type	SQL Query (return single value)
	SQL Query	SELECT reporttitle FROM gl_fs_setup WHERE reportcode=:P18_REPORTCODE1 and cocode=:P18_COCODE
	Source Used	Always, replacing any existing value in session state
	Server-side Condition	Item = Value
	Item	P18_EXISTINGNEW
	Value	EXISTING

(*continued*)

Table 27-2. (*continued*)

Action	Attribute	Value
Create Page Item	Name	P18_REPORTCODE2
	Type	Text Field
	Label	\Code:\
	Region	Financial Statements Parameters
	Start New Row	No
	Column	Automatic
	New Column	Yes
	Column Span	Automatic
	Label Column Span	2
	Server-side Condition	Item = Value
	Item	P18_EXISTINGNEW
	Value	NEW
Create Page Item	Name	P18_REPORTTITLE2
	Type	Text Field
	Label	\Title:\
	Region	Financial Statements Parameters
	Start New Row	No
	Column	Automatic
	New Column	Yes
	Column Span	Automatic
	Label Column Span	2
	Width	50
	Server-side Condition	Item = Value
	Item	P18_EXISTINGNEW
	Value	NEW

27.4 Add an Interactive Grid

Click the Create Page button in the Application Builder interface to add an Interactive Grid region on page 18 using Table 27-3. Select the Form option followed by the Editable Interactive Grid option in the initial wizard screens. In this Interactive Grid, you will specify accounts for each report.

Table 27-3. *Interactive Grid Region*

Action	Attribute	Value
Create Page	Page Number	18
	Page Name	Financial Statements Setup
	Page Mode	Normal
	Existing Navigation Menu Entry	Setup
	Source Type	SQL Query
	SQL Query	SELECT "ROWID", "COCODE", "REPORTCODE", "REPORTTITLE", "FSACCOUNT", "ACCOUNTFROM", "ACCOUNTTO" FROM "#OWNER#"."GL_FS_SETUP" WHERE (reportcode=:P18_REPORTCODE1 or reportcode=:P18_REPORTCODE2) and cocode=:P18_COCODE ORDER BY ACCOUNTFROM
	Primary Key	ROWID
	Select Columns	Select all columns

After creation, enter **Accounts for &P18_REPORTTITLE1.** for the region title.

Modify the new Interactive Grid region on page 18 to incorporate the following amendments:

1. Modify the COCODE column. Set Default Type to Item and enter **P18_COCODE** in the Item attribute.

2. Hide the columns COCODE, REPORTCODE, and REPORTTITLE by setting the Type property to Hidden.

3. Modify the attributes listed in Table 27-4 for the FSACCOUNT
    column.

Table 27-4. *FSACCOUNT Column Attributes*

Attribute	Value
Type	Select List
Heading	Account
LOV Type	Shared Component
List of Values	FINANCIAL STATEMENT ACCOUNTS

4. Modify the attributes listed in Table 27-5 for the ACCOUNTFROM and
    ACCOUNTTO columns.

Table 27-5. *ACCOUNTFROM and*
ACCOUNTTO Column Attributes

Attribute	Value
Type	Popup LOV
Heading	From/To
LOV Type	Shared Component
List of Values	COA ALL LEVELS
Width	45

27.5 Create Validations

Using Table 27-6, create two validations. The first checks for a report code when you
create parameters for a new report. The second prompts you if it finds a code that
already exists in the database.

Table 27-6. *Validation Attributes*

Action	Attribute	Value
Create Validation	Name	Report Code Not NULL
	Type	Item is NOT NULL
	Item	P18_REPORTCODE2
	Error Message	Report Code must be provided for new reports.
	When Button Pressed	SUBMIT
	Server-side Condition	Item = Value
	Item	P18_EXISTINGNEW
	Value	NEW
Create Validation	Name	Check Report Code
	Type	PL/SQL Function (returning Error Text)
	PL/SQL Function	Book_Code\Chapter27\Check Report Code.txt

27.6 Modify Save Interactive Grid Data Process

Modify the default Save Interactive Grid Process as follows:

Attribute	Value
Type	PL/SQL Code
PL/SQL Code	Book_Code\Chapter27\Save IG Data 27.6

27.7 Test Your Work

Execute the following steps to test this segment:

1. Run the segment from the Financial Statement option under the Setup menu. You'll see the segment page as illustrated in Figure 27-1.

2. Select the New option from the radio group to define parameters for a new report.

3. In the Code box, enter **PL01** and type **Profit & Loss Statement** in the Title box.

4. Click the Add Row button to define the first account for this report.

5. In the Account column, select Sales from the select list. Click From LOV and select the 4-REVENUES account from the chart of accounts. Click the To LOV and select the last-selling account (i.e., 40100200002 Sales Return & Discount–Local). By setting these parameters, you specified a range for the sales accounts that will be used in the next chapter to fetch sales figures for the P&L report.

6. Add some more P&L accounts to the tabular form, as shown in Figure 27-1, to complete this setup.

7. Click the Apply Changes button.

8. Using a file named `Balance Sheet Accounts.PNG` in the book's code, create a new report to specify accounts for the Balance Sheet.

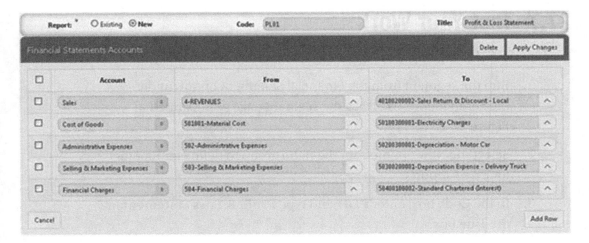

Figure 27-1. *P&L accounts*

27.8 Summary

In this chapter, you laid the foundation for the two most significant financial reports: the P&L Statement and the Balance Sheet. In the next chapter, you will learn how to create these two reports.

CHAPTER 28

Financial Statements

This is the segment that returns the final result of the efforts you have made so far. In this chapter, you will create the Profit and Loss (P&L) and Balance Sheet financial statements. These statements are based on the setup parameters you specified in Chapter 27. The P&L Statement shows the profitability, whereas the Balance Sheet reports on the equities, liabilities, and assets of a business. Combined, these two reports reveal the financial state of an organization.

28.1 Financial Statements Table

The following table was added to the database through the script file to store the two financial statements along with respective notes:

```
CREATE TABLE gl_fs_report
(reportcode varchar2(4), reporttitle varchar2(50), srno NUMBER, fsaccount
varchar2(50), currentbalance number(15,2), previousbalance number(15,2),
percent number(7,2), userid varchar2(50), coname varchar2(50), coyear
number(4), comonthname varchar2(9), calculation number(1), netvalue
number(1), notes number(1), notescode varchar2(11), notestitle
varchar2(50), heading number(1))
```

28.2 Create Page and Page Items

Create a blank page and add the items to it using Table 28-1.

© Riaz Ahmed 2019
R. Ahmed, *Cloud Computing Using Oracle Application Express*,
https://doi.org/10.1007/978-1-4842-4243-8_28

Table 28-1. *Page Attributes*

Action	Attribute	Value
Create Blank Page	Page Number	76
	Name	Financial Statements
	Page Mode	Normal
	Breadcrumb	—Do not use breadcrumbs on page—
	Navigation Preference	Identify an existing navigation menu entry for this page.
	Existing Navigation Menu Entry	Reports
Create Region	Title	Financial Statements Parameters
	Type	Static Content
	Template	Standard
Create Page Item	Name	P76_COCODE
	Type	Hidden
	Region	Financial Statements Parameters
	Source Type	SQL Query (return single value)
	SQL Query	SELECT cocode FROM gl_users WHERE userid=:APP_USER
Create Page Item	Name	P76_CONAME
	Type	Hidden
	Region	Financial Statements Parameters
	Source Type	SQL Query (return single value)
	SQL Query	SELECT coname FROM gl_company WHERE cocode=(select cocode from gl_users where upper(userid)= upper(:APP_USER))

(*continued*)

Table 28-1. *(continued)*

Action	Attribute	Value
Create Page Item	Name	P76_CURRENTFROMDATE
	Type	Hidden
	Region	Financial Statements Parameters
	Source Type	SQL Query (return single value)

	SQL Query	SELECT pfrom FROM gl_fiscal_year
		WHERE cocode=:P76_COCODE and
		        coyear=:P76_CURRENTYEAR
		        and comonthid=1

	Source Used	Always, replacing any existing value in session state
Create Page Item	Name	P76_CURRENTTODATE
	Type	Hidden
	Region	Financial Statements Parameters
	Source Type	SQL Query (return single value)

	SQL Query	SELECT pto FROM gl_fiscal_year
		WHERE cocode=:P76_COCODE AND
		        coyear=:P76_CURRENTYEAR
		        AND comonthid=:P76_
		        CURRENTMONTH

	Source Used	Always, replacing any existing value in session state
Create Page Item	Name	P76_PREVIOUSFROMDATE
	Type	Hidden
	Region	Financial Statements Parameters
	Source Type	SQL Query (return single value)

	SQL Query	SELECT pfrom FROM gl_fiscal_year
		WHERE cocode=:P76_COCODE AND
		        coyear=:P76_CURRENTYEAR-1
		        AND comonthid=1

	Source Used	Always, replacing any existing value in session state

(continued)

Table 28-1. (*continued*)

Action	Attribute	Value
Create Page Item	Name	P76_PREVIOUSTODATE
	Type	Hidden
	Region	Financial Statements Parameters
	Source Type	SQL Query (return single value)
	SQL Query	SELECT pto FROM gl_fiscal_year WHERE cocode=:P76_COCODE AND coyear=:P76_CURRENTYEAR-1 AND comonthid=:P76_ CURRENTMONTH
	Source Used	Always, replacing any existing value in session state
Create Page Item	Name	P76_COMONTHNAME
	Type	Hidden
	Region	Financial Statements Parameters
	Source Type	SQL Query (return single value)
	SQL Query	SELECT comonthname FROM gl_fiscal_year WHERE cocode=:P76_COCODE AND coyear=:P76_CURRENTYEAR AND comonthid=:P76_CURRENTMONTH
	Source Used	Always, replacing any existing value in session state
Create Page Item	Name	P76_REPORTCODE
	Type	Select List
	Label	Code:
	Region	Financial Statements Parameters
	Start New Row	Yes

(*continued*)

Table 28-1. (*continued*)

Action	Attribute	Value
	Column/Column Span	Automatic
	Label Column Span	1
	Template	Required
	Value Required	Yes
	LOV Type	SQL Query
	SQL Query	SELECT distinct reportcode||' - '||reporttitle d, reportcode r FROM gl_fs_setup WHERE cocode=:P76_COCODE
Create Page Item	Name	P76_CURRENTYEAR
	Type	Select List
	Label	Current Year:
	Region	Financial Statements Parameters
	Start New Row	No
	Column	Automatic
	New Column	Yes
	Column Span	Automatic
	Label Column Span	2
	Template	Required
	Value Required	Yes
	LOV Type	SQL Query
	SQL Query	SELECT distinct coyear d, coyear r FROM gl_fiscal_year WHERE cocode=:P76_COCODE ORDER BY Coyear

(*continued*)

Table 28-1. (*continued*)

Action	Attribute	Value
Create Page Item	Name	P76_CURRENTMONTH
	Type	Select List
	Label	\Month:\
	Region	Financial Statements Parameters
	Start New Row	No
	Column	Automatic
	New Column	Yes
	Column Span	Automatic
	Label Column Span	2
	Template	Required
	Value Required	Yes
	LOV Type	SQL Query
	SQL Query	SELECT DISTINCT comonthname d, comonthid r FROM gl_fiscal_year WHERE cocode=:P76_COCODE order by comonthid
Create Button	Button Name	PROFIT_LOSS
	Label	Generate P&L
	Region	Financial Statements Parameters
	Button Position	Copy
	Action	Submit Page
Create Button	Button Name	BALANCE_SHEET
	Label	Generate Balance sheet
	Region	Financial Statements Parameters
	Button Position	Copy
	Action	Submit Page

28.3 Create Interactive Report and Buttons

Using Table 28-2, create an interactive report region to produce the onscreen view of the financial statements.

Table 28-2. *Interactive Report Region*

Action	Attribute	Value
Create Region	Title	&P76_REPORTCODE.
	Type	Interactive Report

	SQL Query	SELECT * from gl_fs_report
		WHERE upper(userid)=upper(:APP_USER) AND
		        notes=0 AND
		           reportcode=:P76_REPORTCODE
		ORDER BY srno

	Template	Standard
Create Button	Button Name	PRINT
	Label	Print
	Region	&P76_REPORTCODE.
	Button Position	Copy
	Action	Submit Page
Create Button	Button Name	PRINT_NOTES
	Label	Print Notes
	Region	&P76_REPORTCODE.
	Button Position	Copy
	Action	Submit Page

Modify the interactive report as shown in Figure 28-1 and save it by selecting the As Default Report Settings option followed by the Primary option.

Account	Current Year	Previous Year	% Change
Sales	249,000.00	175,000.00	42.29
Cost of Goods	0.00	15,500.00	-100
.....Gross Margin	249,000.00	159,500.00	56.11
Administrative Expenses	17,000.00	48,500.00	-64.95
Selling Expenses	60,000.00	3,500.00	1614.29
Financial Charges	500.00	0.00	0
	171,500.00	107,500.00	59.53

Figure 28-1. *The Interactive Report*

28.4 Create Computations

The two financial statements are generated for the selected year (which is treated as the current year) along with comparative figures from the previous year. The computations listed in Table 28-3 are created to evaluate the proper periods from the fiscal year table and are used in the processes created in the next section.

Table 28-3. *Computation Attributes*

Action	Attribute	Value
Create Computation	Item Name	P76_CURRENTFROMDATE
	Point	After Submit
	Computation Type	SQL Query (return single value)
	SQL Query	SELECT pfrom FROM gl_fiscal_year WHERE cocode=:P76_COCODE AND coyear=:P76_CURRENTYEAR AND comonthid=1
Create Computation	Item Name	P76_CURRENTTODATE
	Point	After Submit
	Computation Type	SQL Query (return single value)
	SQL Query	SELECT pto FROM gl_fiscal_year WHERE cocode=:P76_COCODE AND coyear=:P76_CURRENTYEAR AND comonthid=:P76_CURRENTMONTH
Create Computation	Item Name	P76_PREVIOUSFROMDATE
	Point	After Submit
	Computation Type	SQL Query (return single value)
	SQL Query	SELECT pfrom FROM gl_fiscal_year WHERE cocode=:P76_COCODE AND coyear=:P76_CURRENTYEAR-1 AND comonthid=1
Create Computation	Item Name	P76_PREVIOUSTODATE
	Point	After Submit
	Computation Type	SQL Query (return single value)
	SQL Query	SELECT pto FROM gl_fiscal_year WHERE cocode=:P76_COCODE AND coyear=:P76_CURRENTYEAR-1 AND comonthid=:P76_CURRENTMONTH

(*continued*)

Table 28-3. (*continued*)

Action	Attribute	Value
Create Computation	Item Name	P76_COMONTHNAME
	Point	After Submit
	Computation Type	SQL Query (return single value)
	SQL Query	SELECT comonthname FROM gl_ fiscal_year WHERE cocode=:P76_COCODE AND coyear=:P76_CURRENTYEAR AND comonthid=:P76_CURRENTMONTH

28.5 Create Ajax Callback Processes

Open the Shared Components interface. Click Application Processes in the Application Logic section to create two Ajax Callback processes, as listed in Table 28-4. Note that these processes will be called from two different application pages.

Table 28-4. *Ajax Callback Attributes*

Action	Attribute	Value
Create Process	Name	Generate Profit and Loss
	Point	Ajax Callback: Run this application process when requested by a page process.
	PL/SQL Code	Book_Code\Chapter28\Generate Profit and Loss.txt
	Server-side Condition	Current Page Is Contained Within Expression 1 (comma delimited list of pages)
	Expression 1	1,76

(*continued*)

Table 28-4. (*continued*)

Action	Attribute	Value
Create Process	Name	Generate Balance Sheet
	Point	Ajax Callback: Run this application process when requested by a page process.
	PL/SQL Code	Book_Code\Chapter28\Generate Balance Sheet.txt
	Server-side Condition	Current Page is Contained Within Expression 1 (comma-delimited list of pages)
	Expression 1	1,76

28.6 Create Branches

Using Table 28-5, create two branches on page 76 to run the previous on-demand processes. Right-click the Processing node and select Create Branch from the context menu. Set the following attributes for the new branches. The request (APPLICATION_PROCESS) calls the two on-demand processes to generate P&L and Balance Sheet statements along with respective notes. Note that the process name is case-sensitive and must be provided as it was set in the Name attribute in the previous section.

Table 28-5. *Branch Attributes*

Action	Attribute	Value
Create Branch	Name	Generate Profit and Loss
	Point	Processing
	Type	Page or URL (Redirect)
	Target	Type: **Page In This Application**
		Page: **76**
		Request (*under Advanced*):
		APPLICATION_PROCESS=Generate Profit and Loss
	When Button Pressed	PROFIT_LOSS
Create Branch	Name	Generate Balance Sheet
	Point	Processing
	Type	Page or URL (Redirect)
	Target	Type: **Page In This Application**
		Page: **76**
		Request (*under Advanced*): **APPLICATION_ PROCESS=Generate Balance Sheet**
	When Button Pressed	BALANCE_SHEET

28.7 Create Page for Financial Statements Notes

Using Table 28-6, create a blank page and its components. This page is invoked from a link on page 76 (created in the next section) to browse the notes (details) of the selected account.

Table 28-6. *Page for Financial Statements Notes*

Action	Attribute	Value
Create Blank Page	Page Number	77
	Name	Financial Statement Notes
	Page Mode	Modal Dialog
	Breadcrumb	—Do not use breadcrumbs on page—
	Navigation Preference	Identify an existing navigation menu entry for this page.
	Existing Navigation Menu Entry	Reports
Create Region	Title	Notes to the Accounts
	Type	Interactive Report
	SQL Query	SELECT fsaccount, notescode, notestitle, currentbalance, previousbalance, percent FROM gl_fs_report WHERE upper(userid)=upper(:APP_ USER) AND notes=1 AND fsaccount=:P77_ FSACCOUNT ORDER BY notescode
Create Page Item	Name	P77_FSACCOUNT
	Type	Hidden
	Region	Notes to the Accounts

The Notes page should look like Figure 28-2 after completing this chapter.

Financial Statement Notes				✕
▶ ☰ Notes:				
Notes: : Administrative Expenses				
Code	**Title**	**Current**	**Previous**	**% Change**
50200100001	Staff Salaries Expense (Admin)	10,000.00	8,000.00	25
50200100002	Gratuity Expense	0.00	37,000.00	-100
50200200001	Electricity Expense	2,000.00	1,500.00	33.33
50200300001	Depreciation - Motor Car	5,000.00	2,000.00	150

Figure 28-2. *Notes page*

28.8 Create Column Link

Switch back to page 76 to convert the Account column into a link. Click the FSACCOUNT column and set the attributes listed in Table 28-7.

Table 28-7. *FSACCOUNT Column Attributes*

Action	Attribute	Value
Modify Report Column	Type	Link
	Target	Type = Page In This Application
		Page = 77
		Set Items
		Name **Value**
		P77_FSACCOUNT #FSACCOUNT#
		Clear Cache = 77
	Link Text	#FSACCOUNT#

28.9 Enter Vouchers

Using the two files (2015.PDF and 2016.PDF) provided in the book code (Chapter28 folder), create some more vouchers to get a complete picture of the two financial statements. The file 2015.PDF contains a couple of transactions related to expense accounts. These transactions should be posted in the previous year—in other words, 2015. Every time you create or amend an expense or revenue account in the previous year, the temporary year-end (TYE) process must be executed to reflect these amendments in the P&L account. Failing to do so may result in inaccurate financial statements. After posting all vouchers from the two PDFs, switch back to 2015 and execute the TYE process.

28.10 Test Your Work

Execute the following steps to test this part of the application:

1. Invoke it from the Reports ➤ Financial Statements menu.

2. Select PL01-Profit & Loss Statement from the Code list, select 2016 as the Current Year, and select June from the Month list, as illustrated in Figure 28-3 (top). Click the Generate P&L button to execute the corresponding process created in Chapter 28. The interactive report defined under the Parameters region will be populated with the P&L Report. The first column (Account) of this report is presented as a link that you defined in the "Create Column Link" section. This link was created to browse the details behind a selected account. Click the Sales link to see its notes.

3. To test the Balance Sheet Report, switch the code to BS01- Balance Sheet. Keep the year and month parameters as is. To produce an accurate balance sheet statement, you must click both buttons. Click the Generate P&L button first to calculate the profit and loss figures that are reflected in the balance sheet. After clicking this button, the P&L Report will appear in the Interactive Report. Next, click the Generate Balance Sheet button that invokes the corresponding on-demand process and presents the report on your screen.

4. Click the Print button to have a PDF version of the main financial report (shown at the bottom of Figure 28-3) currently displayed on your screen. The Print Notes button produces a PDF carrying the details of the selected report. I've provided all four PDFs in the book code (in the Chapter28 folder).

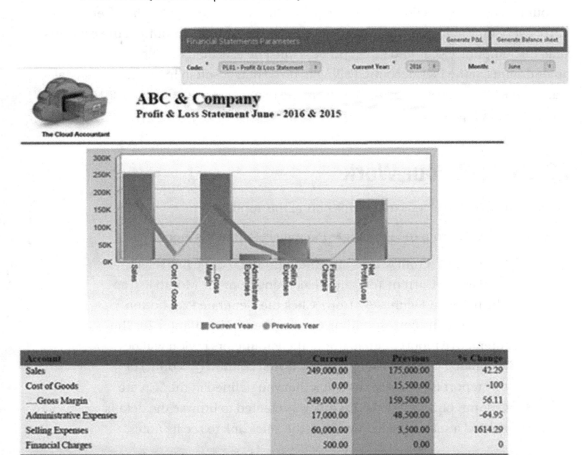

Figure 28-3. *Financial report*

28.11 Summary

The two financial reports you created in this chapter are the most wanted reports by the management of any organization. In the next chapter, you will finish this group with an executive dashboard comprising various analysis charts.

CHAPTER 29

Executive Dashboard

You created the two most vital accounting reports in the previous chapter. With the information provided by these reports, all stakeholders of an organization assess their business health. Among these stakeholders are the business executives who need some more information so that they can evaluate their business at a glance. To satisfy the need of these key stakeholders, you will create an executive dashboard in this chapter to graphically present the information they are looking for.

29.1 Dashboard Table

This segment will use the following table that has already been added to the database through the script file:

```
CREATE TABLE gl_dashboard
(srno NUMBER, accountTitle varchar2(50), currentYear number(15,2),
previousYear number(15,2), userid varchar2(50), ratioTitle varchar2(50),
current_year number(15,2), previous_year number(15,2))
```

29.2 Copy Components to the Home Page

This segment will be created in the Home page (page 1), which already exists in your application. What's more, it uses the same processes and page components used in the previous chapter, which means that you are not required to re-create them. If you look at the bottom part of the two on-demand processes (Chapter 28), you will find three code blocks labeled P&L Account Balances, P&L Ratios, and Balance Sheet Ratios. These are the PL/SQL blocks that relate to this segment. After calculating figures for the two financial statements, these blocks are executed to calculate figures that appear in different charts on the Home page.

© Riaz Ahmed 2019
R. Ahmed, *Cloud Computing Using Oracle Application Express*,
https://doi.org/10.1007/978-1-4842-4243-8_29

Usually you modify a page to add components to it. But this time you are going to learn how to use the Copy to other Page option to copy a whole region along with its components from page 76 to the Home page.

1. On page 76, right-click the region named Financial Statements Parameters and select the option labeled Copy to other Page... from the context menu. Set the attributes listed in Table 29-1. Once finished, edit the Home page where you will see the copied region with all of its components.

Table 29-1. Copy Region

Attribute	Value
To Page	1
Copy Region Items	Yes
Copy Buttons	Yes
Region Name	Dashboard Parameters

2. Click the Dashboard Parameters region on the Home page and change its Type from Static Content to Region Display Selector. Scroll down in the Properties pane and set Region Display Selector to No. Setting the Type attribute to Region Display Selector displays region names in a horizontal list, enabling end users to select one region to display and hide other regions. Only page regions with their Region Display Selector attribute set to Yes will be displayed in the horizontal list.

3. Repeat the previous step to copy the five computations from page 76 to page 1, considering the attributes listed in Table 29-2. After copying these computations, go to page 1 and amend their respective SQL queries by replacing the P76 prefix with P1 to point to the items on the Home page.

Table 29-2. *Copy Computations*

Attribute	Value
Copy Computation	P76_CURRENTFROMDATE ... P76_COMONTHNAME
Target Page	1 (*same for all 5 computations*)
Target Computation Sequence	10 ... 50
Target Item to be Computed	P1_CURRENTFROMDATE ... P1_COMONTHNAME

4. Copy the two branches (Generate Profit and Loss and Generate Balance Sheet, listed in Table 29-3) from page 76 to the Home page. After creation, change the Page attribute (under Target) from 76 to **1** in both branches.

Table 29-3. *Copy Branches*

Attribute	Value
Copy Branch	Generate Profit and Loss
Target Page	1
Target Page Branch Sequence	10
When Button Pressed	PROFIT_LOSS (Generate P&L)
Copy Branch	Generate Balance Sheet
Target Page	1
Target Page Branch Sequence	20
When Button Pressed	BALANCE_SHEET (Generate Balance Sheet)

29.3 Create Regions

Right-click the main Regions node and select Create Region to create two regions (as mentioned in Table 29-4) on the Home page.

Table 29-4. *Region Attributes*

Action	Attribute	Value (Region 1)	Value (Region 2)
Create Region	Title	Profit & Loss Trend	Ratio Analysis
	Type	Static Content	Static Content
	Parent Region	-Select- (*in other words, no parent region*)	-Select-
	Region Display Selector	Yes	Yes

29.4 Create Chart Subregion

This region will display the current year's P&L accounts in a pie chart. To create this region, right-click the Profit & Loss Trend region and select Create Sub Region from the context menu. Set the attributes listed in Table 29-5 for the new region.

Table 29-5. *Subregion Attributes*

Attribute	Value
Title	\<b\>Year&**P1_CURRENTYEAR**.\</b\>
Type	Chart
Parent Region	Profit & Loss Trend
Body Height (*in Template Options*)	240px
Column Span	6
New Node:	
Source Type	SQL Query
SQL Query	SELECT null, accounttitle, **currentyear** FROM gl_dashboard WHERE userid=:APP_USER AND srno BETWEEN 1 AND 11 ORDER BY by srno
Attributes Node:	
Chart Type	Pie

29.5 Create a Hidden Item

The chart to be created later in the chapter (Table 29-7) will display the P&L trend for the previous year. Create the hidden item (as listed in Table 29-6) to assess the previous year value.

Table 29-6. *Hidden Item Attributes*

Action	Attribute	Value
Create Page Item	Name	P1_PREVIOUSYEAR
	Type	Hidden
	Region	Dashboard Parameters
	Source Type	SQL Query (return single value)
	SQL Query	SELECT :P1_CURRENTYEAR - 1 FROM dual

29.6 Copy Chart Regions

Right-click the region Year&P1_CURRENTYEAR. and click the Duplicate option in the context menu. A copy of the existing region will be created under it with the same name. Set the attributes listed in Table 29-7 for the new region, keeping all others as is.

Table 29-7. *Region Attributes*

Attribute	Value
Title	Year&**P1_PREVIOUSYEAR.**
Start New Row	No
SQL Query	SELECT null, accounttitle, **previousyear** FROM gl_dashboard WHERE userid=:APP_USER AND srno BETWEEN 1 AND 11 ORDER BY srno

Duplicate any existing chart, such as Year&P1_PREVIOUSYEAR, and set the attributes listed in Table 29-8. This chart will render the current revenue trend.

Table 29-8. *Revenue Trend Attributes*

Attribute	Value
Title	Revenue Trend
Type	Chart
Parent Region	Profit & Loss Trend
Body Height *(in Template Options)*	320px
Column Span	6
New Node:	
Source Type	SQL Query
SQL Query	SELECT null, accounttitle, currentyear, previousyear FROM gl_dashboard WHERE userid=:APP_USER AND srno=1
Attributes Node:	
Chart Type	Column

Make a duplicate of the Revenue Trend chart and set the attributes listed in Table 29-9. As the name implies, this chart will show the expenses trend.

Table 29-9. *Expenses Trend Attributes*

Attribute	Value
Title	Expenses Trend
Start New Row	No
New Node:	
SQL Query	SELECT null, accounttitle, currentyear, previousyear FROM gl_dashboard WHERE userid=:APP_USER AND (srno=3 or srno=8 or srno=9 or srno=10)

Make a copy of Revenue Trend and set the attributes listed in Table 29-10. This region will show the gross profit ratio. All the regions from this point will be placed under the Ratio Analysis region.

Table 29-10. *Gross Profit Ratio Attributes*

Attribute	Value
Title	Gross Profit Ratio
Parent Region	Ratio Analysis
Body Height (*in Template Options*)	320px
Column Span	4
New Node:	
SQL Query	SELECT null, accounttitle, current_year, previous_year FROM gl_dashboard WHERE userid=:APP_USER AND **srno=50**

Make a duplicate of Gross Profit Ratio to create Operating Profit Ratio. Incorporate the attributes listed in Table 29-11 in the new region.

Table 29-11. *Operating Profit Ratio Attributes*

Attribute	Value
Title	Operating Profit Ratio
Start New Row	No
New Node:	
SQL Query	SELECT null, accounttitle, current_year, previous_year FROM gl_dashboard WHERE userid=:APP_USER AND **srno=52**

Make a duplicate of the Operating Profit Ratio region to create the Net Profit Ratio region with the distinctions listed in Table 29-12.

Table 29-12. *Net Profit Ratio Chart Attributes*

Attribute	Value
Title	Net Profit Ratio
New Node:	
SQL Query	SELECT null, accounttitle, current_year, previous_year FROM gl_dashboard WHERE userid=:APP_USER AND **srno=53**

Make the Current Ratio region from Gross Profit Ratio considering the distinctions listed in Table 29-13.

Table 29-13. *Current Ratio Attributes*

Attribute	Value
Title	Current Ratio
Sequence	100
New Node:	
SQL Query	SELECT null, accounttitle, current_year, previous_year FROM gl_dashboard WHERE userid=:APP_USER AND **srno=60**

Using Table 29-14, make the Net Working Capital region from Operating Profit Ratio.

Table 29-14. *Net Working Capital Attributes*

Attribute	Value
Title	Net Working Capital
Sequence	110
New Node:	
SQL Query	SELECT null, accounttitle, current_year, previous_year FROM gl_dashboard WHERE userid=:APP_USER AND **srno=62**

Make the Quick Ratio region from Net Profit Ratio, using Table 29-15.

Table 29-15. *Quick Ratio Attributes*

Attribute	Value
Title	<b>Quick Ratio</b>
Sequence	120
New Node:	
SQL Query	SELECT null, accounttitle, current_year, previous_year FROM gl_dashboard WHERE userid=:APP_USER AND **srno=63**

29.7 Test Your Work

Click the application title The Cloud Accountant on the top of your screen to see the Home page. Select BS01-Balance Sheet, 2016, and June for Code, Current Year, and Month, respectively. Hit the Generate P&L button. Once the page gets refreshed, hit the Generate Balance Sheet button. If Region Display Selector is set to the default Show All option, then you'll see all 10 charts on your screen. Click the option Profit & Loss Trend in the region selector. This action will hide the 6 charts created under the Ratio Analysis region. Similarly, if you click the Ratio Analysis option (Figure 29-1), the 4 charts created under the Profit & Loss Trend region will be hidden.

Figure 29-1. *Ratio analysis charts*

29.8 Summary

The charts you added to the Home page provide insight into an organization's financial status. Here you learned how to create different types of analyses for management. In the next chapter, you will create a feedback module that allows interaction among application users.

CHAPTER 30

Application Feedback

This segment is added to create interaction among the application administrator and its users. It allows end-users to communicate application issues to the application administrator. It consists of a form and a report. The form is created for the users to input their feedback, while the report is used by the application administrator to browse the issues added through the form.

30.1 Application Feedback Table

The following table and sequence were created through the script file to store application feedback received from the users of the application:

```
CREATE TABLE gl_feedback
(feedbackID NUMBER, TS timestamp default sysdate, custName varchar2(50),
custEmail varchar2(100), custFeedback varchar2(4000), CONSTRAINT GL_
FEEDBACK_PK PRIMARY KEY (feedbackID) ENABLE)

CREATE SEQUENCE gl_feedback_seq
```

30.2 Create Feedback Input Form

Using Table 30-1, create a new page. On the first wizard page, select Form, and on the next page, select Form on a Table.

© Riaz Ahmed 2019
R. Ahmed, *Cloud Computing Using Oracle Application Express*,
https://doi.org/10.1007/978-1-4842-4243-8_30

Table 30-1. *Page Attributes*

Action	Attribute	Value
Create Page	Table/View Name	GL_FEEDBACK (table)
	Page Number	300
	Page Name	Application Feedback
	Page Mode	Normal
	Region Title	Application Feedback
	Navigation Preference	Do not associate this page with a navigation menu entry.
	Primary Key Type	Select Primary Key Column(s)
	Primary Key Column 1	FEEDBACKID
	Source for Primary Key Column 1	Existing Sequence
	Sequence	GL_FEEDBACK_SEQ
	Select Columns	Select all columns
	Branch here on Submit	1
	Cancel and Go To Page	1

Modify the feedback page as follows:

1. Change the Type value of the timestamp field (P300_TS) to Hidden. Set the Default Type value of this item to PL/SQL Expression and enter **sysdate** as the value for the PL/SQL Expression attribute to store the current system date for each feedback.

2. Set the labels of the three text items to **Customer**, **Email**, and **Feedback**. Also set Template to Required and Value Required to Yes for these three Text Field items.

3. Select the P300_CUSTFEEDBACK item and set its Height attribute to 20 lines.

4. Click the process named Process Row of GL_FEEDBACK on the Processing tab. Type **Thank you very much for providing your valuable feedback** in the Success Message box.

30.3 Create Feedback Report Page

Next, create an Interactive Report page to display a list of all feedback entered through page 301. This report allows an administrator to see and reply to the users' feedback. Click the Create Page button. Select the Report option on the first wizard screen followed by the Interactive Report option. Set the attributes as listed in Table 30-2.

Table 30-2. *Feedback Report Page Attributes*

Action	Attribute	Value
Create Page	Page Number	300
	Page Name	Feedback Report
	Page Mode	Normal
	Navigation Preference	Identify an existing navigation menu entry for this page.
	Existing Navigation Menu Entry	Reports
	SQL Query	SELECT * FROM gl_feedback

Modify the feedback report page by changing the column headings as shown in Figure 30-1 (bottom).

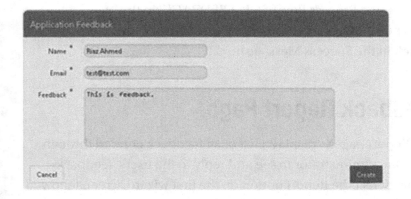

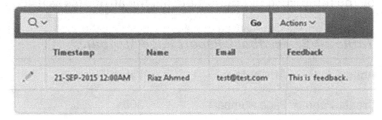

Figure 30-1. *Feedback report page*

30.4 Test Your Work

Click the Feedback link in the navigation bar to run the Feedback Input form. Enter your name, e-mail address, and some text, such as **This is feedback** (shown earlier at the top of Figure 30-1), and click the Create button. An acknowledgment message will appear, indicating that your feedback was received. Expand the Reports menu and click the Feedback option to see the feedback you just saved.

30.5 Summary

In this chapter, you learned how application users can interact with each other to discuss application issues. In the next chapter, you will create a small footprint of the application that is accessible on smartphones.

CHAPTER 31

Application Security

Before you go live with an application, it is important to apply proper security measures. One of the most basic forms of protection that any web application must have is the enforcement of an authentication and authorization policy. *Authentication* deals with identifying users to the application; you've already implemented it in this application using a custom authentication scheme: a username and password. *Authorization* is the process of assessing whether the authenticated user is privileged to access certain data or perform a particular action. Recall that you have already laid the foundation of application authorization in Chapter 6, where you specified the application segments to which you want to apply authorization. Then, you created user groups and provided them with the appropriate application access privileges. In this chapter, you will create a bunch of authorization schemes to protect your application. These schemes will be created to protect menus, pages, buttons, and processes.

31.1 Authorization Schemes for the Main Menu

First you will create some authorization schemes to control access to the menu options of your application. Note that you have 9 main menus and 26 submenu options in the application. These all need to be protected through individual authorization schemes to prevent unauthorized application access. In this section, you will create authorization schemes for the nine main menu options. The submenu options will be controlled through the Page Access authorization scheme, as listed in Table 31-4 later in this chapter. Use the table to create these authorization schemes. The code for all these schemes is the same except for the menu name that must be changed for each menu item. For example, the menu name Home (presented in bold in the following code) should be replaced with the word **Setup** for the Setup menu, **Select** for the Select menu, and so on. Go to Shared Components, select Authorization Schemes under the Security section, and click the Create button. Select the From Scratch option in the initial wizard screen and set the remaining attributes as indicated in Table 31-1.

325

© Riaz Ahmed 2019
R. Ahmed, *Cloud Computing Using Oracle Application Express*,
https://doi.org/10.1007/978-1-4842-4243-8_31

Table 31-1. *Application Menu Authorization Scheme*

Attribute	Value
Name	Home
Scheme Type	PL/SQL Function Returning Boolean
PL/SQL Function Body Book_Code\Chapter31\ Menu Authorization.txt	DECLARE

```
DECLARE
    Vadmin varchar2(1);
    Vallow varchar2(1);
BEGIN
    SELECT admin INTO Vadmin FROM gl_users
    WHERE upper(userid)=upper(:APP_USER);
    IF Vadmin = 'N' then
        SELECT allow_access INTO Vallow FROM
        gl_groups_detail
        WHERE segmentType='Menu' AND
                segmentID=(select segmentID from
                                gl_segments
                                where
                                segmentTitle='Home (Menu)' and
                                segmentType='Menu')
                                AND
                                groupID=(select groupID
                                from gl_users
                                where upper(userid)
                                =upper(:APP_USER));
        if Vallow='Y' then
    return true;
        else
    return false;
        end if;
    ELSE
        return true;
    END IF;
EXCEPTION
    WHEN NO_DATA_FOUND THEN RETURN FALSE;
END;
```

(continued)

Table 31-1. (*continued*)

Attribute	Value
Identify error message...	Home authorization scheme violated
Validate authorization scheme	Once per session

Create the remaining menu authorization schemes, as listed in Table 31-2. Replace segmentTitle='Home (Menu)' in the PL/SQL code with the corresponding menu.

Table 31-2. *Menu Authorization Schemes*

Name	PL/SQL Code Text	Identify Error Message...
Setup	segmentTitle='Setup (Menu)'	Setup authorization scheme violated
Select	segmentTitle='Select (Menu)'	Select authorization scheme violated
Transactions	segmentTitle='Transactions (Menu)'	Transactions authorization scheme violated
Utilities	segmentTitle='Utilities (Menu)'	Utilities authorization scheme violated
Reports	segmentTitle='Reports (Menu)'	Reports authorization scheme violated
Closing	segmentTitle='Closing (Menu)'	Closing authorization scheme violated
Feedback	segmentTitle='Feedback (Menu)'	Feedback authorization scheme violated

After creating the menu authorization schemes, go to Shared Components and in the Navigation section select Navigation Menu ➤ Desktop Navigation Menu; then click the Home menu entry, select Home for the Authorization Scheme attribute, and click the Apply Changes button. This action will attach the Home authorization scheme to the Home menu. Repeat this step for the remaining menu options (as shown in Table 31-3) including Feedback in the desktop navigation bar.

Table 31-3. *Menu Items and Associated Authorization Schemes*

Menu Entry	Authorization Scheme
Home	Home
Setup	Setup
Select	Select
Transactions	Transactions
Utilities	Utilities
Reports	Reports
Closing	Closing
Feedback	Feedback

31.2 Test Menu Authorization

Test the menu authorization schemes you just implemented using the following steps. Make sure you have created the Clerks group (in Chapter 7) and the user John (in Chapter 8) who is assigned to this group. Recall that the Clerks group was created without any application access privileges.

1. Log in to the application using John's credentials and see that no application menu is available to this user.

2. Log in using the application's administrator credentials.

3. From the Setup menu, select the User Groups option and then select the existing Clerks group. Allow access to the Select, Transactions, Utilities, Reports, and Feedback menus for this group.

4. Log in again as user John and observe that the five menu options are now accessible.

31.3 Authorization Schemes for Application Pages

After controlling the main menu access, your next task is to control the application pages that are usually executed through submenus (except for the pages associated with the Select and Transactions menus). Go to Shared Components and create the authorization scheme listed in Table 31-4. This is the only authorization scheme that controls access to all application pages. The text defined in the "Identify error message" attribute is a custom message with a link to take the unauthorized user to the Select page (page 30), which is usually granted to every application user.

Table 31-4. *Authorization Scheme for Application Pages*

Attribute	Value
Name	Page Access
Scheme Type	PL/SQL Function Returning Boolean
| PL/SQL Function Body Book_Code\Chapter31\Page Access Authorization.txt | ```
DECLARE
  Vadmin varchar2(1);
  Vallow varchar2(1);
BEGIN
  SELECT admin INTO Vadmin FROM gl_users
  WHERE upper(userid)=upper(:APP_USER);
  IF Vadmin = 'N' THEN
    SELECT allow_access INTO Vallow FROM gl_
            groups_detail
    WHERE pageID=:APP_PAGE_ID AND
          segmentType='Page' AND
          groupID=(select groupID from gl_users
                    where upper(userid)=upper
                    (:APP_USER));
    if Vallow='Y' then
      return true;
    else
      return false;
    end if;
  ELSE
    return true;
  END IF;
EXCEPTION
  WHEN NO_DATA_FOUND THEN RETURN FALSE;
END;
``` |
| Identify error message… | You are not authorized to view this page!
 Click <a href="f?p=&APP_ID.:30:&SESSION.">here</a> to continue. |
| Validate authorization scheme | Once per page view |
```

31.4 Test Page Authorization

Execute the following steps to test the page authorization:

1. Edit page 54 (Copy COA). Click its root node (page 54: Copy COA). In the Properties pane, scroll down to the Security section and set the Authorization Scheme attribute to Page Access. Save the modification.

2. Log in to the application using John's credentials. Expand the Utilities menu and click the Copy Chart of Accounts option. The message defined in the previous table will appear and prevent you from accessing the page. Click the "here" link, which will take you to the Select page.

3. Log in as the application administrator and allow John's group to access the Copy COA segment.

4. Log in again using John's credentials and click the Copy COA menu option. This time the page will come up.

5. Using step 1, apply the Page Access authorization scheme to all application pages except for the global and login pages.

31.5 Authorization Schemes for Buttons

An application page usually contains several different types of items. From a security point of view, the most significant item is the button, which is used to send a request for further processing. You used six buttons (Save, Create, Modify, Delete, Display, and Print) to handle different processes in this application. In this section, you will control the application processes by creating some authorization schemes for these buttons. Table 31-5 creates an authorization scheme to control the Save buttons on all application pages. Use this table to create schemes for the remaining five buttons, replacing the text *itemRole='Save'* with the appropriate button name.

Table 31-5. *Button Authorization Schemes*

Attribute	Value
Name	Save
Scheme Type	PL/SQL Function Returning Boolean

PL/SQL Function Body Book_Code\Chapter31\Button Authorization.txt	DECLARE
	  Vadmin varchar2(1);
	  Vallow varchar2(1);
	BEGIN
	    SELECT admin INTO Vadmin FROM gl_users
	    WHERE upper(userid)=upper(:APP_USER);
	    IF Vadmin = 'N' THEN
	      SELECT allow_access INTO Vallow FROM
	          gl_groups_detail
	      WHERE pageID=:APP_PAGE_ID AND
	          itemRole='Save' AND
	          groupID=(select groupID from
	              gl_users where
	              upper(userid)=upper
	              (:APP_USER));
	     if Vallow='Y' then
	      return true;
	     else
	      return false;
	     end if;
	    ELSE
	     return true;
	    END IF;
	EXCEPTION
	  WHEN NO_DATA_FOUND THEN RETURN FALSE;
	END;

Identify error message…	Save button authorization scheme violated
Validate authorization scheme	Once per page view

31.6 Test Buttons Authorization

Execute the following steps to test the button authorization:

1. Edit page 54 (Copy COA). Click the Copy button. In the Properties pane, scroll down to the Security section, and set the Authorization Scheme attribute to Save. Save the modification.

2. Log in using John's credentials and run the page from the Utilities menu. The button has vanished from the page, because John's group was created without any application access privileges.

3. Log in as the application administrator and grant access to this button to the Clerks group.

4. Log in as John. This time the Copy button on the Copy COA page will be visible.

5. Using the file Apply_Authorization_Schemes.xlsx provided in the Book Code Chapter31 folder, apply the relevant authorization schemes to all buttons on all application pages.

Note   When applying security to a button, remember to also apply equal security constraints to the process that is invoked when the button is clicked. For example, the Authorization Scheme attribute of the Copy COA process on page 54 must be set to Save. This way, the process is also attached to the authorized scheme that matches the button to avoid access-control vulnerability.

31.7 Summary

In this chapter, you learned how to apply strong security on each component of your APEX application. Either through an application page or a button on that page, you can control user access to all application components.

31.8 Conclusion

The main objective behind this book was to give you insight into developing business applications for the cloud. You can develop such applications and offer them to the business community under the software as a service model. Now, why should you use Oracle APEX for this? It's simply because Oracle APEX is a rising platform in which you can develop Internet-facing applications rapidly, as you have just experienced. Besides being a rapid application development tool, Oracle APEX offers many features that are lacking in other web development platforms. The new IDE has made the process of application development much easier than ever before. The strong navigation features found in APEX cannot be created that easily in any other development tool. Using the shared components, you can use application components and logic in more than one place. Eye-catching charts and mobile integration are among many other features offered by this platform for rapid application development, but the most important one is the use of less code that is required when you are implementing custom application logic. In addition, everything can easily be handled through the built-in features. In a nutshell, Oracle APEX has made the life of developers significantly easier. With this development platform, you can create any kind of business application instantly to meet the challenges of today's ever-evolving business world.

Index

A

Access privilege, 66
ACCOUNTFROM and ACCOUNTTO
    column attributes, 291
Accounting
    analysis, financial information, 4
    Cloud Accountant general ledger
        project, 6–7
    general ledger system, 5–6
    profitable organization, 4
    suppliers, 4
    systems, 4
    tasks, 4
Accounts table, 283
Add dynamic action, cost center, 97
Ajax Callback processes, 304–305
APEX Accounts scheme, 7
API, 176
Application-building process
    company setup, 18–19
    page creation, 18–19
    tables, creation, 17
Authentication, reset password, 83–84
Authorization schemes
    application pages, 330
    buttons, 331–332
    main menu, 325–328
    test buttons, 333
    test menu, 328–329
    test page, 331

B

Balance Sheet, 283
    financial statements, 295
Bank reconciliation
    definition, 223
    display transactions, 225–227
    interactive grid region attributes,
        229–230
    opening form, 227–228
    page, 230–231
    page attributes and parameters
        form, 224–225
Bank reconciliation report
    format, 237
    highlight rule, 237
    interactive report
        attributes, 236
    output, 238
    parameters form
        attributes, 234–235
    PDF version, 238
    process attributes, 236
    table creation, 233
Bank transactions
    COCODE column, 221
    creating page, 220
    opening banks region
        attributes, 220–221
    page attributes, 220
    steps, test, 222

335

© Riaz Ahmed 2019
R. Ahmed, *Cloud Computing Using Oracle Application Express*,
https://doi.org/10.1007/978-1-4842-4243-8

Printed in the United States
By Bookmasters